Book of NATURE PROJECTS

ELIZABETH P. LAWLOR

with illustrations by Pat Archer

STACKPOLE BOOKS

Published by
STACKPOLE BOOKS
5067 Ritter Road
Mechanicsburg, PA 17055
www.stackpolebooks.com

Printed in the United States of America

10 9 8 7 6 5 4 3 2 1

First edition

Additional text by Jim Conrad, Tim Herd, Diana Lawton, Rebecca Lawton, and Susan Panttaja

Additional illustrations by Jim Conrad, Irene Guidici Ehret, and Patrice Kealy

Cover design by Wendy Reynolds

Library of Congress Cataloging-in-Publication Data
Lawlor, Elizabeth P.
  Book of nature projects / Elizabeth Lawlor. — 1st ed.
    p. cm
  ISBN-13: 978-0-8117-3480-6
  ISBN-10: 0-8117-3480-3
  1. Science projects. 2. Science—Experiments. I. Title.

Q182.3.L336 2008
507.8—dc22

2007044202

CONTENTS

INTRODUCTION   1

1. AROUND THE HOUSE   5

2. CLOSE TO HOME   35

3. IN THE GARDEN   65

4. AT SUNDOWN   91

5. IN WINTER   115

6. IN THE WEATHER   145

7. IN ROCKS AND WATER   169

8. AT THE SEASHORE   209

INTRODUCTION

This book is for people who want to find out about the plants and animals that live in areas close to them. It is concerned with knowing and doing, organized with background information and a hands-on project to help discover more about each subject. It is for the young, for parents, for students, for teachers, for retirees, for all those with a new or renewed interest in the world around us. Getting started as a naturalist requires a friendly, patient guide. This book is intended to be just that.

Each chapter introduces you to a certain area in which to explore familiar—and not so familiar—plants and animals. You will learn about each organism's unique place in the web of life and the most fascinating aspects of its lifestyle. Each chapter also provides you with activities—things you can do to discover for yourself where to find each living thing, what it looks like, and how it behaves and survives.

Start with any part or chapter in this book. For instance, if you are planning a vacation to the Outer Banks of North Carolina, begin reading about life at the seashore, and pack any items you may need to explore. Consider keeping a field notebook to record your observations.

The intent of this book is to be only a beginning for you. When you have gone into the woods, traversed the rocky plains, or stopped by your backyard garden, and when you have experienced these places throughout the year, you have gone beyond the knowledge contained in this book. Once you have started, you will have the best guide of all—nature itself.

What to Bring

To become fully involved in the hands-on activities suggested in this book, you'll need very little equipment. Your basic kit requires only a few essentials. Start with the field notebook. I generally use a spiral-bound, five-by-seven-inch memo book. Throw in some ballpoint pens and pencils. Since several of the explorations will involve taking some measurements, a six-inch flexible ruler or tape measure is another essential. Include a small magnifier or hand lens. Nature centers generally stock good plastic lenses that cost less than five dollars. You could also get a battery-operated, hand-held, lighted magnifier (30X) moderately priced at about ten dollars. You may also want to have a bug box—a small, see-through acrylic box with a magnifier permanently set into the lid. It's a handy item for examining such creatures as snow fleas, mole crabs, ants, etc. With it you can capture, hold, and study the creature without touching or harming it. Keep a penknife in your kit as well. You'll use it for slicing into cacti, prying open seeds, and innumerable other tasks.

All the basic kit contents easily fit into a medium-sized Ziploc bag, ready to carry in a backpack, bicycle basket, or the glove compartment of a car.

Basic Kit

field notebook	penknife
ruler	pens and pencils
magnifier	small sandwich bags
bug box	

Although not essential, a pair of binoculars adds to the joy of discovery. Today there are many very good, inexpensive binoculars on the market. A camera is another useful tool for studying plants and animals.

For a few activities you'll need a bucket, glass jars with lids, a watch with a second hand, sticks, string, and a compass. You will also want a three-ringed loose-leaf notebook. Here you can enter, in an expanded form, the information collected in the field. As you make notes, you'll have an opportunity to reflect on what you saw and to think through some of the questions raised during your explorations. Consult your reference books and field guides for additional information.

You will understand as you read and investigate how fragile these communities of living things can be. You will inevitably encounter the effects of man's presence. Perhaps you will become concerned in specific, practical ways. This kind of concern is the way to make a difference for the future of the environment. We still have a long way to go.

1

AROUND THE HOUSE

Examine the Anatomy of a Fern

Modern ferns are descendants of the giant ferns that dominated the landscape long ago. Today, ferns are smaller and more retiring, preferring to live in nooks and crannies of rocky hillsides or sheltered in the shade along a streambank. People who have grown to love ferns in their natural setting frequently want to cultivate them indoors. How can you replicate the familiar surroundings of ferns in the wild in your home? What kinds of ferns will tolerate the low humidity and high heat of our homes?

Ferns lack flowers, fruits, and seeds, which sets them apart from other plants.

1. **Frond, or leaf blade.** The flat, green leaf blades, or fronds, vary in size and shape. Fronds are usually compound, with leaflets attached along a rachis. The size and shape of fronds vary from species to species.
2. **Leaflet.** The leaflets, or pinnae (singular: pinna), are divisions of a compound leaf.
3. **Subleaflet, or pinnule.** Subleaflets are subdivisions of leaflets.
4. **Lobe, or pinnulet.** Lobes are subdivisions of pinnules.
5. **Teeth.** Teeth are serrations along the edges of the pinnae, pinnules, or pinnulets.
6. **Rachis.** The rachis is the backbone of the frond and is the continuation of the stalk supporting the leaflets. It resembles the midrib of a simple tree leaf.
7. **Stalk.** The stalk, or stipe, provides support below the rachis and above the roots.
8. **Rhizome, or rootstock.** Rhizomes are horizontal stems that lie on the surface of the soil or just below it.
9. **Roots.** Roots are thin, threadlike, sometimes wiry structures that anchor the plant and absorb water and minerals from the soil. They grow from the rhizomes.

Make a Fern Terrarium

A terrarium is a tiny greenhouse that will allow you to enjoy ferns throughout the year. To create one, you will need some simple and easily obtained materials.

1. Wash a wide-mouthed gallon jar thoroughly with very hot water, then wash it again and allow it to dry.
2. For drainage, line the bottom of the jar with a layer of gravel or small chunks of clay from broken pots to a depth of about one inch.
3. Add about one-quarter inch of charcoal—this will absorb the gases that decaying vegetation in the soil will produce.

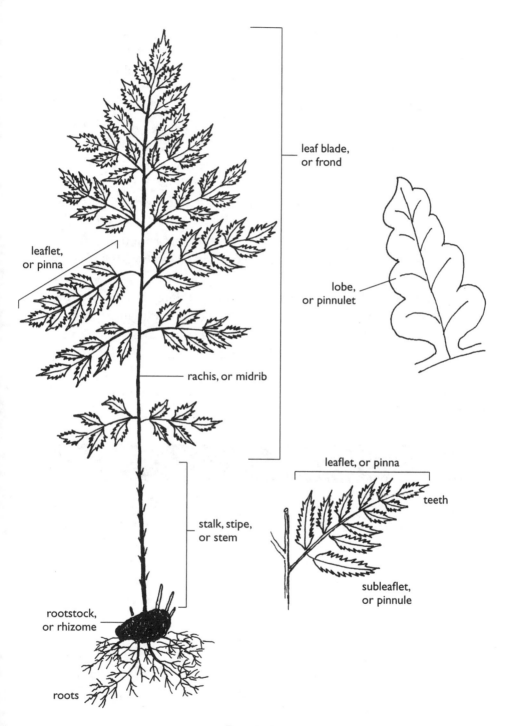

leaf blade, or frond

leaflet, or pinna

lobe, or pinnulet

rachis, or midrib

leaflet, or pinna

teeth

stalk, stipe, or stem

subleaflet, or pinnule

rootstock, or rhizome

roots

Fern anatomy

4. At a nursery or supermarket, purchase a small bag of sterile potting soil, and add it to the jar to a depth of about two inches. The soil needs to be light and airy (potting soil usually contains loam for this purpose).

5. Ferns best suited for a terrarium are small and slow-growing, such as the fragile fern (*Cystopteris fragilis*) and common polypody (*Polypodium virginianum*).

6. Put your terrarium near a window where it will receive northern light—direct rays from the sun will prove deadly. You can also use artificial light by substituting one or more fluorescent light bulbs for this light. The bulbs should be eight to twenty inches from the incubators, and you should keep the light on for about fourteen hours each day. Experiment to find out what conditions are best for your ferns.

7. The amount of water needed will vary depending on the size of the terrarium, where it is located, and the type of ferns planted. You do not want the soil too wet or too dry. If the ferns look healthy, you are probably providing the right amount of water.

8. As the plants need some air, only partially cover the top of the wide-mouthed jar with a small plate made of glass or plastic.

Pot a Cactus

Cacti belong to a group of plants called succulents, which means juicy or full of water. The ability to store water in their leaves or stems is a trait that separates succulents from other plant groups. Cacti have certain characteristics that set them apart from other succulents such as agave, sedum, and aloe. For example, most cacti do not have leaves. They store water in their green stems, which are also their food factories. The notorious spines of the cactus grow out of areoles, white cushions that look like tiny patches of cotton on the stems.

Cacti make great house and patio plants, requiring little watering and scant fertilization. The warm temperatures and dry air in many homes provide ideal conditions for these desert-loving plants. And don't worry about being bored with only a few choices; there are thousands of different kinds of cacti. Never take them from the wild; buy them from legitimate growers or visit a nursery or greenhouse that specializes in these fascinating survivors.

With such a wide variety of cacti available, you must get information on potting for each species. What kind of container is best for a particular cactus? Will it grow better in a wide or narrow pot? If possible, visit a nursery that specializes in cacti, and see what criteria the experts use to select an appropriate pot size.

Almost any kind of container will work for cacti as long as some basic needs are met. The container must provide adequate drainage so that the soil will remain loosely packed and well aerated. Plastic pots are lightweight, nonporous, and relatively inexpensive. Metal cans from your recycling bin are another practical choice. When using a container that lacks drainage holes, put a layer of clay shards or small stones in the bottom of the pot.

1. When you have selected an appropriate container, make sure it is clean. Unless the pots are new, scrub them well, and rinse them in a solution of ten parts water and one part liquid bleach to remove any mold, mildew, pest remains, or other undesirable material left from previous plantings.

2. To transplant the cactus into your new pot, wear a pair of heavy gloves, preferably leather, to avoid getting stabbed by the spines. Do not try to pull the cactus out of the pot with unprotected hands. You can use a pair of kitchen pasta tongs to lift the cactus out of its old pot, or make a strap of folded newspaper long enough to wrap around the body of the cactus, secure the free ends of the strap in one hand, and use the paper sling to lift the cactus from its container. If the soil in the old pot is slightly wet, you should be able to lift the cactus out easily.

3. Place the cactus in the new pot. Pour soil around the roots, being careful not to damage them. Continue adding soil to the pot, leaving about an inch of space at the top. This will help avoid spillage when watering the plant. A recipe for making your own soil mix is simple. It requires one part sand (not from a beach, due to the salt content), one part garden soil, and one part peat moss.

4. Some cactus growers suggest covering the top of the soil with a layer of gravel. This prevents the soil from caking up around the plant's roots. They also suggest that you do not water the cactus for a few days after transplanting. Keep it out of direct sun to allow the roots to recover in case they were damaged during the transplanting process.

Propogate Cacti

You can add to your cactus collection by taking cuttings. A cutting often produces an improved shape, especially if the growth pattern of the parent plant has become distorted in some way. Be sure to wear heavy gloves and use a sharp knife. Some cutting suggestions are found in the illustrations.

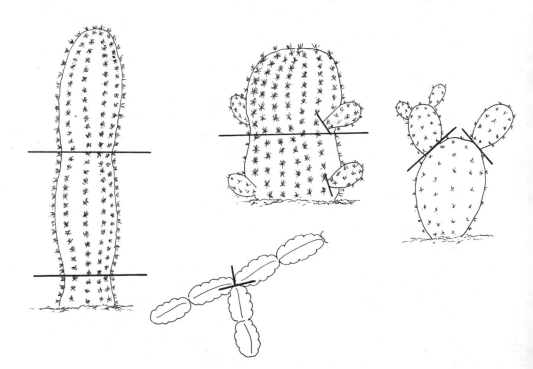

It is best to take cuttings from a natural separation point.

1. Place the cuttings in a cool, dry area, avoiding direct sunlight, until the wounds have hardened. Depending on the size of the cut, the drying process may take from a few days to several weeks.
2. Next you'll want to plant your cuttings in a commercial cactus soil mixture or sand. Before planting, test the drainage of the soil by running water through the pot; it should drain quickly. If drainage is poor, you can add pebbles to the soil mix.
3. Be sure the cuttings stand upright. To achieve this, you will have to experiment with planting them at different depths in the soil.
4. Water the cuttings immediately after planting. Too much water is the primary reason for rooting failure, as it causes root rot, so avoid soggy soil. Allow the soil to become totally dry between waterings, but do not let it remain dry for as long as three or four days. For indoor cacti, the drying time may be as short as twenty-four hours.
5. You will have the best results if you make the cuttings during the natural growing season. In most cases, this is during warm weather.

Graft Cacti

When grafting, you attach a stem cut from a plant you want to improve, called the scion, to the root or stem of a vigorous, closely related cactus, called the stock. The best time for this procedure is during the spring or early autumn, when there is sufficient sap flowing. The cactus you select for the stock must have a healthy root system. A good candidate has uniform color and is firm to the touch, not soft or mushy. It's suggested that the stock and the scion be of the same diameter, but a somewhat smaller scion will work as well. The scion will retain its own characteristics but will get its nourishment from the stock's root system.

1. Using a clean, sharp knife, cut the scion and the stock straight across, on the horizontal, as indicated in the diagram. It's suggested that you bevel the cut edges of the scion and the stock to prevent shrinkage.
2. Press the cut areas of the two pieces together firmly to remove any air that might interfere with the grafting process, and secure them with a rubber band.

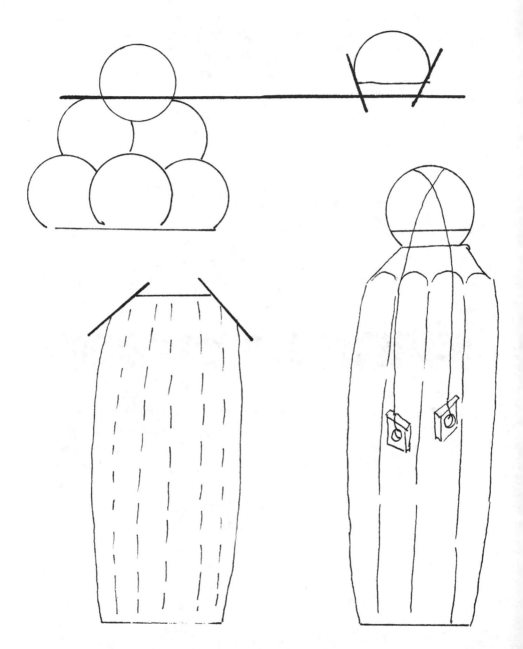

Thick, round scions call for a flat graft, which is the simplest graft.

3. Keep the grafted cactus out of direct sunlight, and don't water it until you notice the parts beginning to grow together. This may take about four weeks. Cacti that are rounded, such as the members of the *Echinocactus* genus, are best suited for this type of graft. Because of its small size, the hedgehog cactus (*Rebutia* spp.) is another good candidate for the stock, and *Gymnocalycium* spp. make a good scion.

4. Keep a record of what you did and how it worked. How does the grafted cactus appear? Does it produce any young sprouts, called offsets? If a cactus produces offsets, detach, plant, and enjoy them.

Grow Potatoes from Seed Potatoes

The most common potatoes are white, red, and russet. These are collectively called white or Irish white potatoes. These are the potatoes commonly eaten baked, boiled, mashed, and made into french fries and chips.

Make a trip to the produce section of a market and buy a few each of white, red, and russet potatoes. Which of these potatoes is most common in your market? At home, examine the characteristics that identify each of these types of potatoes. What is the color of the skin? How would you describe its texture—is it smooth or rough? Does it have a pattern on it? Describe the shapes of the potatoes. Are they round, oval, or oblong? Cut the potatoes in half. Examine the flesh of each kind of potato. Describe it. What similarities do you notice? Differences?

If you want to grow a potato the way commercial growers cultivate them, you will need to have a seed potato. Finding one is not difficult. Sometimes all you need to do is look in a recently bought bag of potatoes, and you will see a few potatoes that are beginning to sprout. If a potato has been in your cabinet for a while, you may discover some strange yellowish shoots and some long, threadlike strands (the rhizomes) growing from it. This is what is known as a "seed potato." It is so called because it contains all the necessary ingredients to produce potatoes identical to itself.

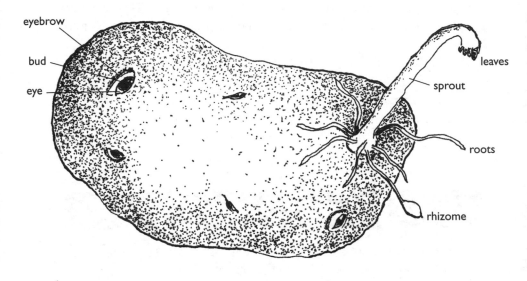

eyebrow

bud

eye

leaves

sprout

roots

rhizome

A sprouting potato

1. Once you have obtained such a potato, cut off several pieces with two or three eyes on each. Cut two or three more pieces that have no eyes.
2. Using a large flowerpot for each piece, plant them in soil to a depth of about three inches. Use sterile potting soil, which can be bought in a nursery or supermarket. How long does it take the sprouts to poke through the soil? Did all your potato pieces grow stems?
3. When a plant has become tall and leaves are present, remove it from the pot, along with the ball of soil. You will see underground rhizomes, and maybe even a tiny potato or two. Look for the original piece of seed potato. How has it changed since you planted it?
4. If you want the plant to continue to grow, replant it in a larger pot or outdoors to allow room for more growth. You might eventually be able to eat the potatoes you grow.

Study Daddy Longlegs

The cool nights and warm days of autumn bring daddy longlegs out of hiding, and this is the best time for a productive arachnid hunting season. Daddy longlegs are not as easy to track down as spiders; most of the time they just appear. To find a daddy longlegs, look in a garage or barn, on the porch or patio, or even in your house. You might find them running along the tops of shrubs and other plantings around your house or among the cobwebs that tend to accumulate in basements and garages. When trapping a daddy longlegs, be sure your container is large enough to accommodate its long, wispy limbs.

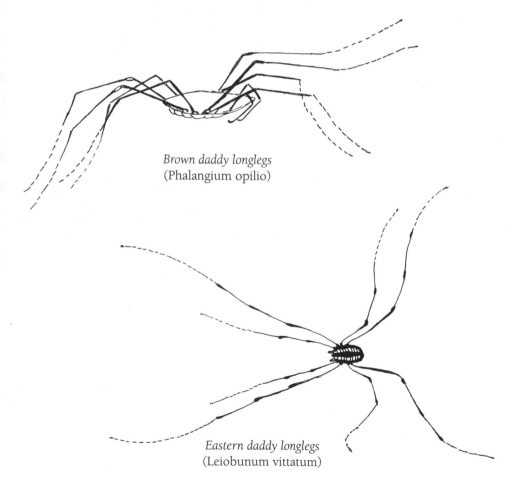

Brown daddy longlegs
(Phalangium opilio)

Eastern daddy longlegs
(Leiobunum vittatum)

There are several kinds of daddy longlegs. The one you are most likely to find around the house is the brown daddy longlegs (*Phalangium opilio*). It is small, with a reddish brown body that may reach a quarter inch. It has two eyes on black turrets. Although its eyes see only shadows, one eye scans to the right while the other eye looks left. It is not very fussy about living in places that we have disturbed. It is even comfortable in places we have made quite messy.

1. Put two or three daddy longlegs in a small, eight-ounce jar. Observe them for a period of time. What do they do?

2. Now put them in a large jar with enough room for each to move freely. How do they behave under these conditions? Do the daddy longlegs stay close to each other, or do they seem to spend most of the time separated? How long did it take for them to settle down? How long do they stay in this settled position?

3. When the daddy longlegs were put in the smaller jar, you probably noticed that they "played dead" after they ran around the jar for a short time. This is called the "narcotic effect." When you move them to a larger jar, they revive almost immediately and become quite active.

Construct a Longlegs Terrarium

In order to observe daddy longlegs more closely, you can keep one on a temporary basis in a five- or ten-gallon terrarium.

1. Add a few inches of soil and some decaying leaves. If you collect these materials from a woodland or garden, they will contain enough tiny soil organisms to feed the daddy longlegs for a period of time.

2. Daddy longlegs require little water. Most of what they need they will take from the soil. Keep it moist by using a spray bottle.

3. Cover the terrarium with plastic wrap or a piece of cardboard. Puncture ventilation holes in this covering.

4. Do not put the terrarium with its captive in direct sunlight. Heat will build up to dangerous levels, putting the daddy longlegs in serious danger of drying out and dying.

5. Daddy longlegs often prey on each other, so it is not advisable to keep more than one in a container for an extended period. You can introduce another and leave it for a short time while you make some observations. How does the original tenant behave in the presence of the newcomer?

Monitor Longlegs Activities

1. If you touch a daddy longlegs, does it scurry away, play dead, or not change its activity at all? How does the daddy longlegs respond to a loud noise? A bright light in a dark room?
2. Daddy longlegs are equipped with a pair of jaws that can tear food. In front of the first pair of legs is a pair of pedipalps, jointed appendages that hold the soft food while a pair of jawlike structures pulls the food into the mouth. Put a daddy longlegs on your hand along with a drop of water or some food. You might see its mouthparts groping as it searches for the food or water.
3. Touch the daddy longlegs' second pair of legs with a soft object, such as a piece of cotton, as they wave about. Let the legs touch a small piece of cooked, chopped meat. How does the daddy longlegs respond to these objects?

Measure Longlegs Speed

Anyone who has seen a daddy longlegs in motion will agree that they are fast runners, but just how fast they travel is not generally known.

1. On a patio or wide driveway, release the daddy longlegs near the center of the pavement.
2. When it starts to run, begin timing. A stopwatch is good for this, although a wristwatch with a second hand can do the job.
3. Use a tape measure to determine how far it traveled in fifteen seconds and thirty seconds.

4. Repeat this several times. What is its average speed per minute? Does it travel in a straight line? You may have to try this several times to become accustomed to the daddy longlegs' behavior and speed.

Study a Praying Mantis

Mantises may be found from midsummer through October or November. If you are extremely lucky, you might find a mantis inside your house. Although they are sometimes found resting on a windowsill, screen door, or plant on the patio, usually mantises are discovered by accident in their natural environment.

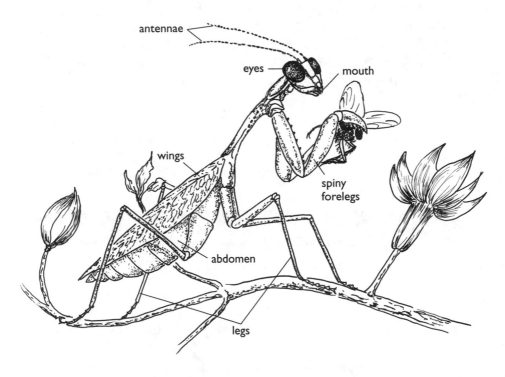

antennae

eyes

mouth

wings

spiny forelegs

abdomen

legs

Anatomy of a praying mantis (Mantidae family)

It is relatively easy to capture these slow-moving insects. An insect net would be helpful but is not necessary because you can usually scoop the mantis up with your hands. Be gentle. The mantis will not bite you, but if you handle it roughly, you can expect to get a pinch from its powerful forelegs.

If you cannot find any mantises, you may be able to purchase them from an organic gardening store or biological supply house, although they may be available only at certain times of the year.

Mantises are more helpful when left outside, where they will eat plant-eating insects, but if you want to explore mantis behavior more closely, you can keep one as a pet.

1. A clear plastic container with a lid makes a satisfactory cage, but be sure to make ventilation holes in the lid. A fish tank will work as well, but you will need a cover. You can make an adequate lid by attaching wire mesh to a frame that fits securely on the tank. Gallon glass jars are not suitable for a mantis because the diameter of the jar is not large enough to allow the insect to move about freely. You can always purchase a small container from a pet store, which you can keep for observing other small animals.

2. Do not line the bottom of the cage with sand, soil, or any other covering because the insects you provide for food will find an effective hiding place. Add a sturdy plant stem with some green leaves for the mantis to use as a perch. Two twigs are usually enough; the mantis can get tangled in the plant material if you add too much to the container.

3. One way to secure food for your mantis is to set up an insect trap. Put some raw meat in the bottom of a jar, and insert a funnel into the mouth. The funnel should fit into the mouth of the jar but not drop into it. Leave the jar outdoors. Among the insects your trap will attract are flies and beetles.

4. Crickets are easy to trap with your hands, but their glossy coating makes them slippery. A medium-sized jar also works well. Pop the jar over the cricket, and slip your hand or a three-by-five index card over the mouth of the jar. Since you will need more than one cricket, keep a larger jar on hand for your captives.

5. You can supply your mantis with water by spraying the sides of the container. One investigator reported feeding a mantis with an eye dropper; can you train your mantis to drink water from one?

6. Observe the mantis for several days. How many times did you see the mantis on the plant? On the lid? If you have added twigs from different plants, which kind does the mantis seem to prefer for a perch? Or does it prefer to hang on to the lid rather than the twigs you provided? Keep a record of your observations.

Examine Ants

Ants come in a variety of colors: black, brown, red, yellow, green, and combinations of these. They also display a dramatic range in size. One species of parasitic ant, which lives within the walls of nests made by larger ants, is only one-twenty-fifth of an inch long, whereas the dinosaur ants of Peru measure over an inch in length. Our more familiar carpenter and field ants measure somewhere in between.

The best way to find an ant is to sit down in the grass or on a decaying tree stump; the ants will soon find you. The large black, brown, or sometimes light reddish carpenter ants are easiest to examine. These ants usually live in the wood of dead trees or the wood of old houses. Capture one and put it into a bug box. Don't worry about taking your captive away from the colony. You will put it back where you found it when you're finished.

1. Find out whether you have trapped an ant or an ant look-alike. Is your creature's body divided into three segments? Can you see its head, chest (thorax), and abdomen as three distinct divisions? If you can see a waist between the chest and abdomen, then it is probably an ant and not a termite. Look at its antennae. Are they straight or do they have an elbow? If they have an elbow, your insect is an ant.

2. Make little piles of small fragments of food, such as meat, cake, sugar, or seeds. How long does it take one ant to find your food supply? What happens next? How many return together to the food source? How long did it take from the time you noticed the

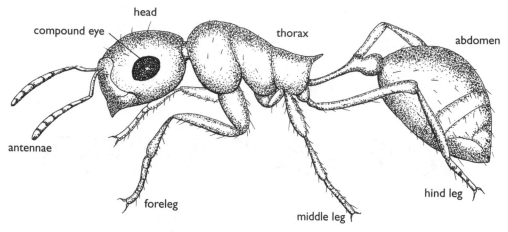

Anatomy of a typical ant (Formicidae family)

first ant until other ants were there? What kind of food did the ants carry away first?

3. To discover something about the way ants live, you need to find a nest. How many openings are there in the nest? How far apart are they? What compass direction do the openings face? How are these openings used by the ants? Is the mound made with loosely packed sand or soil? Is the top thatchlike, made of tiny twigs and grass? How tall is it? What is its diameter? What is the distance around the base of the nest? How close is this nest to others? Are nearby nests occupied by the same kind of ant?

4. Find a mound and mark the place with some sort of flag. Make some notes about the characteristics of the mound. Return to the nest in a day or two. Are there any changes in the shape or size of the nest? Are there other changes? Is there a change in the level of activity from one day to another? Has the temperature changed considerably since your last visit? How does a rain shower change the shape of the nest?

5. Find a decaying tree stump or tree limb lying on the woodland floor. Look for the large, black carpenter ants nearby. Pull off a piece of loose bark and you will probably find a colony of carpenter ants living in a maze of galleries, halls, and rooms.

   Look for worker ants. These are the immature, wingless females. They feed and clean the queen. Can you find her?

6. Other female ants are nurses. They care for the larvae and pupae. Can you find ant larvae and pupae? The pupae of some species are naked and helpless. When viewed with a magnifier, their tiny parts are visible. The pupae of other kinds of ants are wrapped in cocoons and are often mistaken for grains of rice.

Examine Ant Trails

Ants use different strategies to find their way back to their colony. The most common strategy is a scent trail on the ground marked by pheromones that the ant secretes.

When working with ants, it's a good idea to wear gloves, as any ant may bite. Look around your yard, driveway, and sidewalk for a colony of ants.

1. If you see ants following one another outside the nest, all going along the same path, rub your finger across the path. What happens to the parading ants? How do the ants coming along on the path behave? Do they get back on the trail? How long does it take for successive ants to restore the path? Do they have to find the food source first?

2. Put a teaspoonful of honey or syrup about three feet away from the nest, and place four pieces of cardboard around it so that any trail over the cardboard will lead the ants to the honey. Watch the ants as they move from one place to another. Is their path a straight line? How do they use their antennae to follow the scent trail (a chemical path) laid down by the first ants that found the food?

3. Wait until there are about thirty to forty ants traveling to and from the nest. Now turn the cardboard that is closest to the nest 45 degrees from the sweet. What happens?

4. Next turn the cardboard 180 degrees from the original position. What do the ants do? How do ants new to the trail behave? Record their behaviors in your notebook. Try this with other ants in other locations. Compare your results. What did you find out?

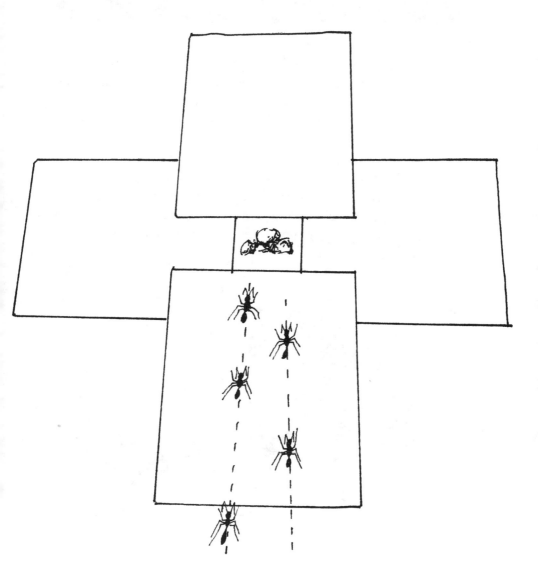

This setup will help you study ant trails.

Observe Ladybugs

Ladybugs have six legs and three body parts (head, thorax, and abdomen), and scientists agree that they are insects. Within that classification, however, ladybugs are not grouped with the "true bugs." The true bug order, Hemiptera, includes such insects as assassin bugs and giant water bugs. Ladybugs belong to the group of insects called beetles, the order Coleoptera. Many other beetles are well known, such as Japanese beetles, weevils, and fireflies, but none shares the popularity of the ladybug. It may surprise you to know that there are more than 350,000 beetle species worldwide. This number is about 40 percent of all insect species. Even more surprising, there are more than 5,000 species of ladybugs around the world, and 370 of those species live in North America.

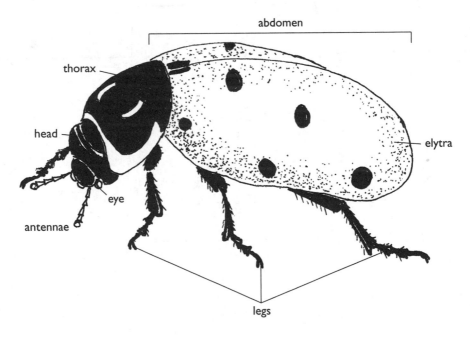

Anatomy of a ladybug

Ladybugs can be found in a variety of places. In the early spring, you may even find them inside the house, perhaps walking along a windowsill.

1. You will need a jar with a lid or a piece of plastic wrap or aluminum foil that you can secure over the mouth with a rubber band. Whichever cap you intend to use, poke a few holes in it for ventilation.

2. To capture a ladybug, put a three-by-five index card in its path. Without hesitation, the ladybug will climb onto it and continue its walk. From here it is easy to coax the ladybug into the jar. If you find a ladybug on a plant, put the mouth of the jar under the leaf or twig it's on, gently tap the supporting foliage, and it will tumble into the jar.

3. With the help of a hand lens, you can discover a great deal about ladybugs. What color is your ladybug? Does it have spots, blotches, or stripes? If so, how many? How are the markings arranged? Are the colors in the wings or in the wing covers, or are both similarly colored?

4. Examining the ladybug carefully, how many body parts do you see? Can you identify the head, thorax, and abdomen? The head and thorax together are about one-fourth of the total length of the ladybug. The rest of the ladybug body is made up of the shiny wing covers, called elytra, as well as the abdomen, antennae, and legs. How many antennae are there? Are they as long as the legs? As long as the thorax is wide?

5. How many legs are there? How does the ladybug use its legs when walking? Are the legs on one side moved forward first, followed by the legs on the other side, or does it move its legs alternately?

6. How does your ladybug hold its wings when it's not flying? When ladybugs are resting, their wings are folded up and covered by the elytra most of the time. Sometimes you will see the tips of the wings sticking out from under the wing covers. When you release it, watch it when it takes flight. Can you see what it does with the wing covers while it's in flight?

Raise Ladybugs in Your Home

In your observations of ladybugs, you likely will find one of the most infamous plant pests—aphids, also known as plant lice. Aphids are among the choice foods for ladybugs. Look for them on the leaves, stems, and flowers of various plants.

1. Find a plant with aphids on it.
2. Make a cage for the plant out of fine wire mesh.
3. Add ladybugs to the plant.
4. Put the cage in a bright location, but not in direct sunlight. In time, the ladybugs will mate and lay eggs.
5. You can observe the development of the ladybugs from eggs to larvae to adults.
6. The newly developed ladybugs will need food. You can supply the hungry beetles with aphids by cutting infested stems from other plants and placing the stems in the cage with the developing ladybugs.

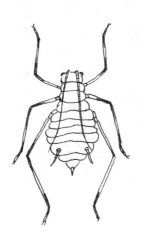 

Aphids may or may not have wings, but all make a hearty meal for ladybugs, which have been known to eat as many as a hundred aphids in a day.

Live-Trap a House Mouse

Observing wild animals is a difficult task requiring knowledge of the animal, stealth, and patience. Mice that live with us can be active at any hour of the day or night. This habit may give you the opportunity to locate a nest, although their tendency to be secretive can make sighting them difficult. You usually realize you are sheltering house mice when you find their tiny, black waste pellets in the kitchen, basement, attic, or garage.

You can learn a great deal about mice by observing them. Since observing mice on the loose can be difficult, you might want to try trapping one in a live trap. You can buy these nonlethal traps at hardware stores. Among the popular brands are Havahart and Victor Live Catch. Many pet stores also sell mice, which are a domesticated strain of *Mus musculus*.

A hamster cage makes a good home for your mouse. Your mouse will also need a water bottle, which may come with the cage. If you've captured a house mouse or wild mouse, this setup makes fine temporary housing, but you should release the mouse back into the wild when you have completed your observations.

The house mouse (Mus musculus)

Map Mouse Movements

Since scientists cannot observe animals all day, every day of the year, they use a system of observing the animals for short periods of time, called sampling. You can learn about certain behaviors of your mouse through sampling. You will need a timekeeper, recorder, and observer to carry out this investigation.

1. Obtain a box approximately 25 inches long by 33 inches wide by 24 inches high. The box must be large enough to allow the mouse to move freely, and the walls must be high enough that the mouse cannot escape.

2. Mark the center of the box with a circle, and write the number "1" in the circle. This is the starting place for the mouse. For record keeping, use a sheet of paper the same shape as the bottom of the box. Draw a circle with this number "1" at the center of the record sheet.

3. Introduce the mouse into the box by placing it on the circle. After ten seconds, draw a circle marked with a "2" on your map to indicate the new position of the mouse. Use an arrow to indicate the direction the mouse is facing.

4. Continue noting the mouse's position in this way every ten seconds for about five minutes, numbering each new location sequentially. Then put the mouse back in its cage.

5. For the next trial, construct a shelter from an 8½-by-11-inch piece of cardboard, folding it to create a three-sided tent. Place it at one end of the box, and place some food at the other end.

6. Put the mouse in the circle at the center of the box, and record its movements as you did during the first investigation. What did you discover? Were your findings what you expected?

7. After several days, repeat these investigations. Are the findings the same or different? Does it seem to matter if you stay well back from the observation area? Would the mouse behave differently if you went away and used a video camera mounted to view the behavior? Field scientists also have to consider how their presence might affect their observations of animal behavior.

8. Now analyze your record sheets. Where are the most circles placed? How many are in the corners of the box? In the center of the box? Do you see a pattern in the mouse's movements? Did the mouse tend to seek the wall of the box? The corners? The open space? Did the mouse spend much time in the shelter?

Characterize Cats

Cats come in a wide assortment of colors, sizes, and shapes, not to mention temperaments. Some are playful, and others are aloof. Some are pedigreed, and others are not. A pedigreed cat is one that has a traceable ancestry. It has specific physical characteristics and behaviors that distinguish it from other breeds.

Watch for different cat varieties when you travel away from home. You may want to ask a veterinarian or contact a local cat association for some help with your search. Books at your local library may aid you in identification. A camera would be helpful to get a record of a breed that you do not recognize immediately.

A cat will illustrate one of three body types. The lithe body type is seen in Siamese and Abyssinian cats. These are slender, lightly built cats with long bodies, slim legs, narrow shoulders and rump, and wedge-shaped heads.

The cobby cat has a stocky body, broad shoulders and rump, short, stubby legs, and a flat face. Persian cats have this body type.

The semiforeign body type is represented by the American short-hair cat and Devon rex. These cats have a sturdy muscular build, intermediate leg length, medium rump and shoulder width, and slightly rounded heads.

1. Compare the eating habits of the cat with those of a dog. Does the cat gobble its food the way a dog does? Does either animal clean the bowl or leave some for a snack later in the day? What does each of the animals do if there is food it doesn't like? Design and carry out an investigation that will help you find out what foods your cat prefers. Feed the cat at the same time in the same place every day,

pupil in darkness   pupil in medium bright light   pupil in bright sunlight

The effect of light on a cat's pupil

use the same bowl each time, and feed it the same amount of each test food.

2. Our pupils react to changes in the amount of light in our environment. When we are in dim light, our pupils become larger, but in bright light, they become smaller. Do cats' pupils respond the same way? Cats' eyes react to dimming light before sunrise and after evening twilight. In a dimly lit room, shine a flashlight at the eyes of a cat, and you will see the pupils change from large and round to a narrow slit. These adaptations help the cat see in various light intensities.

3. A cat can look at something for a very long time without blinking. Use a watch with a second hand or a stopwatch to time a cat as it stares at an object. How long does it go without blinking? Have a friend stare at something as long as he or she can without blinking. Compare the stare times of the cat and your friend. What did you find out? Try this with other cats and other people. Are the results similar or different?

4. How does a cat respond when you hold it in front of a mirror where it can see its image? Compare the reactions of the cat with those of a dog of a similar age. What did you find out?

5. To determine whether your cat favors its right or left paw, put some food that your cat especially likes into a clean wide-mouthed jar. Place the open jar on its side on the floor. Be sure the food is close enough to the opening that the cat can reach it with a paw. Which paw does the cat use to scoop out the food? Try this several times. Does it always use the same paw? What did you discover?

6. Watch a cat as it walks. Do the feet on the left or right side move together, or do the feet alternate from one side to the other? You may not notice that the cat's four feet almost step in each other's tracks. A cat can walk on a path that is only two inches wide. How is this an advantage for the cat?

Distinguish Dogs

Early dogs looked very different from the dogs of today, although German shepherds and some other breeds do resemble the wolves from which they descended.

A breed is defined as a group of animals bred by humans to possess certain inheritable qualities, including a uniform appearance, that distinguish it from other members of the same species. Today the American Kennel Club divides American breeds into seven different classes, based on various roles dogs play in our lives.

Sporting dogs. Alert and active, these dogs are selected for hunting. Members of this group include spaniels, setters, and pointers.

Terriers. These are high-energy dogs, often described as feisty. Airedales, cairn terriers, Welsh terriers, and West Highland white terriers are a few representative breeds.

Hounds. An acute sense of smell has led to the nickname "scent hounds" for some members of the group. Others are prized for their vision and are called "sight hounds." Beagles, bloodhounds, dachshunds, and whippets are in this group.

Working dogs. These dogs serve us by guarding property, pulling sleds, or rescuing people. Newfoundlands, Portuguese water dogs, Bernese mountain dogs, boxers, and Doberman pinschers are among the working dogs.

Herding dogs. They are known for their ability to herd other animals, controlling their movements. The size of herd animals is unimportant. The dogs do the job as well with cows as they do with ducks. Shetland sheepdogs, border collies, Pembroke Welsh corgis, and collies are in this group.

Toy dogs. These small dogs are often called lapdogs. Members of this group are toy poodles, miniature pinschers, Chihuahuas, and Italian greyhounds.

Nonsporting dogs. The poodle, Lhasa apso, Boston terrier, bulldog, and shih tzu are members of this group. Many of us have wonderful dogs that are not members of any AKC classification. These mixed-breed dogs are "special blends," and perhaps they deserve a category of their own.

There are basically two types of dog behavior. One kind is genetically inherited, such as the need to satisfy hunger, and the other is learned. Dogs that have been trained to come on command are displaying learned behavior. Observe your dog carefully for about a week, and make a list of those behaviors that are inherited and those that are learned.

1. Go to a wide-open space, such as a field or park, and stand at one end of the field without your dog knowing you are there. Have a friend blindfold your dog and take it about a hundred yards away, then remove the blindfold. Wave to your dog, but don't call its name. How does it respond? Call the dog's name. Does its response change? Does it show learned behavior by responding to your call, or does it simply ignore your voice and illustrate instinctive behavior by smelling the grass in the vicinity of your friend?

2. Sheepdogs (herding dogs) have a 180-degree field of vision. The field of vision for the Pekingese is 5 to 10 degrees, and that of terriers is 20 to 30 degrees. Design an investigation that will give you some idea of your dog's field of vision.

3. Unlike our eyes, those of the dog are designed to help it see best in dim light. In a dark room, shine a flashlight into your dog's eyes. What color do you see? How do you explain the color?

4. Observe your dog breathing normally when at rest. How would you describe its breathing? Time the number of respirations in a minute. How does that compare with your own number of respirations in a minute?

5. What happens to the dog's breathing when you introduce a new, unexpected odor, such as perfume on a piece of cloth? Observe the dog's behavior. What does it do with its nose? This behavior is

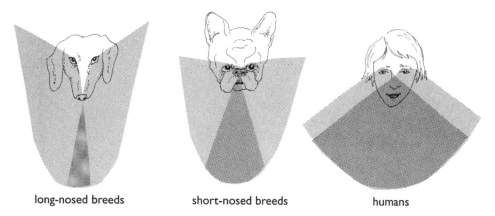

long-nosed breeds   short-nosed breeds   humans

The variation in the shape of dogs' heads causes differences in eye placement and thus influences their fields of vision.

called sniffing. How does it differ from the ordinary breathing you observed?

6. Experts tell us that the dog's sense of smell is far superior to its sense of taste. Offer your dog a piece of food. What is the first thing the dog does when offered the food? Does the dog taste your offering immediately, or does it sniff the food first?

2

CLOSE TO HOME

Identify Deciduous Trees

More than a thousand kinds of deciduous trees live in North America. The activities that follow will help you become better acquainted with deciduous trees and the way they work. A good place to begin your tree study is in your backyard, a public park, or a golf course. Limit your search to a few trees at a time. It is easier to identify a tree by examining its leaves than by examining its bark, flower, or shape, so begin your study when the trees are in leaf.

1. The first step is to become familiar with the variety of leaf shapes and sizes. Pick a few obviously different trees. Are the leaves oval, heart-shaped, or elliptical? Are they lance-shaped or egg-shaped? Are they diamond or triangular? Do any of the leaves have lobes? Are the edges serrated (toothlike), doubly serrated, or smooth? Are the edges wavy? You may find that one shape or edge pattern is more common.

2. How are the leaves arranged on the twig? Are they opposite each other or are they alternately placed? Are they whorled, radiating out like spokes from a wagon wheel? Which is the most common leaf arrangement on the trees in your sample? Are the leaves

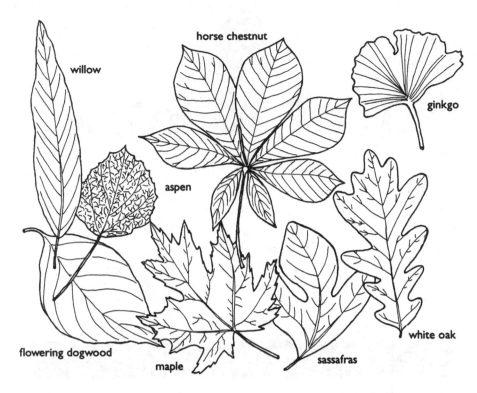

A tree can be most easily identified by the shape of its leaves. (Individual leaves are not drawn to scale.)

simple? Do they have one blade attached to the leaf stem? Or are they compound? Are there a few or several leaflets attached to the leaf stem? Are the surfaces of the leaves smooth or rough? Are they hairy? Is the color or texture of the leaf the same or different on top and bottom surfaces?

3. Make a tree portfolio by taking pictures of different trees throughout the year. Your collection should include photographs of trees, flowers, fruits, leaves, and barks. You may think that all bark looks alike, but you'll be surprised that you can identify a tree by the pattern of its bark. Include the location of the tree and the date you took each picture in your portfolio.

Measure the Height of a Tree

1. To measure the height of a standing tree all you need is a cardboard triangle, a measuring tape, and enough space around the tree to make your observations. Make your triangle from a square piece of cardboard with sides of one foot. Cut the square from one corner to the opposite corner. You will only need one of the triangles to measure the height of your tree. The ground around the tree whose height you want to measure needs to be reasonably level for this method to work.

2. Walk away from the tree until you think you may be where the top of the tree would land if you cut it down. Face the tree. Hold the triangle so that one of the short sides is parallel to the ground and the other short side is parallel to the trunk of the tree.

3. Place the tip of the triangle that's closest to you at eye level. Pretend the long edge is a gunsight and you are shooting at the topmost twig. If you are too close to the tree, the sight will aim at a lower branch and you will have to walk backward until you see the tip of the tree in your "sight." If you are too far away, you will be aiming at the sky. In this case walk toward the tree until you see the top of the tree at the tip of the long side. When you are sighted just right (be sure to keep the bottom edge of the triangle parallel to the ground), you will be standing almost one tree height from the tree.

4. With your tape measure, measure the distance from the base of the tree to the spot where you are standing (A). Add to that your height from the ground to your eye (B). The sum of these two numbers will equal the approximate height of the tree, that is, A + B = H.

5. Is there a relationship between the height of the tree and the number of main branches on the tree? Using the same method as outlined above, find the height of several trees of the same species. Then count the main branches on each tree. It's easiest to count them if you stand under the tree and look up. Record the count for each tree.

Collect Twigs

1. Twigs come in a variety of sizes, shapes, colors, and textures. Make a collection of twigs, starting with beech, oak, hickory, and maple, if you can find them. How many colors did you find among your twigs? Were the twigs straight, zigzag, or curved? Use the outline below to study additional twig traits.
2. **Terminal bud.** Is it large? Sticky? Pointed? Rounded or cigar-shaped? Is it smooth or hairy? Watch the tree through the spring and find out what develops from this end bud.
3. **Side buds.** How do they resemble the terminal bud?
4. **Lenticels.** Are they present on each of your twigs? Is there any pattern to their arrangement? How far back from the tip of the twig can you find them?
5. **Leaf scar.** Compare the leaf scars on each of your twigs.
6. **Terminal bud scale scar.** This is the point where the bud scales of the terminal bud were attached. The distance between each ring,

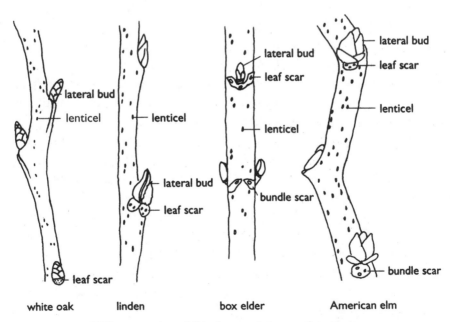

white oak   linden   box elder   American elm

Different species exhibit characteristic growth patterns.

which looks like a rubber band around the twig, is equal to one year's growth. In what year did your twig grow the most? Look at other twigs the same age on the same tree. Did they also grow the most in that year?

7. **Pith.** In each type of tree, twigs show a pattern of pith unique to the tree type. Cut a cross section of twig and examine the pith. If it is star-shaped, it is probably an oak, poplar, or hickory twig. If the pith is circular, you probably have a twig from an elm.

Explore Pine Trees

The pine family is a very large group of conifers. Most of its members are familiar Christmas tree species. The pine family includes larches or tamaracks (*Larix* spp.), spruces (*Picea* spp.), hemlocks (*Tsuga* spp.), Douglas-firs (*Pseudotsuga* spp.), true firs (*Abies* spp.) and, of course, pines (*Pinus* spp.).

Winter is a good time to begin making observations, when pines stand out among the skeletons of deciduous trees.

1. The members of the pine family make excellent windbreaks. You can discover this for yourself on any cold and windy winter day. Visit a dense grove of conifers, standing on all sides of the trees. What differences did you notice? Did you notice any difference in the sound of the wind?

2. Visit a Christmas tree market and ask permission to forage for pieces of trunk, discarded branches, and twigs. Inspect the branches on one tree. Is the bark at the tip the same as in the middle of the branch? Examine the trunk. Is the bark at the top the same as it is at the base? Find a tree that is lying down. How are the branches arranged on the trunk? Are they opposite each other? Are they alternately placed, as in a series of steps? Do three or more branches grow from the same level on the trunk, like spokes of a wagon wheel? Is this growth pattern the same for the twigs?

3. Since a whorl of branches forms on the tree each year, you can find out how old pines and spruces are by counting the number of whorls. Don't forget to count the whorls made by branches that

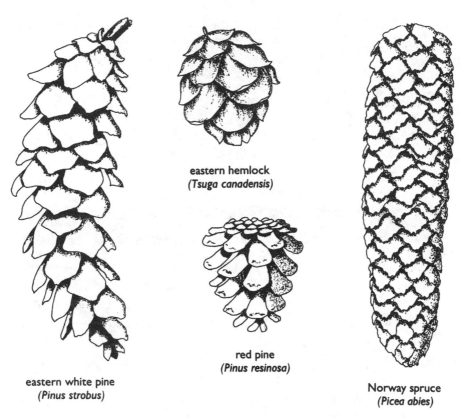

eastern hemlock
(*Tsuga canadensis*)

red pine
(*Pinus resinosa*)

eastern white pine
(*Pinus strobus*)

Norway spruce
(*Picea abies*)

Cones are seed-bearing structures unique to each pine tree.

have been removed. The evidence for these branches will be scars on the trunk. What is the age of the youngest Christmas tree? The oldest? What's the average age?

4. What is the average age of trees of one species in your neighborhood? What age is the oldest tree of this species? The youngest? How can you find out what the life span of that species is?

5. Another method used to determine the age of a tree is counting the rings in a piece of trunk. Cut segments of trunk from a tree that has been thrown away after the holidays. Get disks from the lower and upper portions of the trunk. Lightly sand these disks to see the rings better. Using a disk from the lower trunk, determine the age of the tree. Compare the number of rings at the base of the tree with those at the top. Measure the width of each ring to determine how much the tree grew each year. Is this the same for both disks?

Count Seeds

Seeds are the relatively new invention of a large group of highly specialized plants. Seed-bearing plants first appeared during the Triassic period some two hundred million years ago. The earliest seed plants were the gymnosperms, ancestors of our present-day pines, spruces, and firs. Gymnosperm comes from a Greek word meaning "naked seed." This refers to the fact that seeds of cone-bearing plants develop on the scales of the cones and not within the protective wall of a plant ovary.

About fifty million years after the appearance of coniferous trees, angiosperms—or flowering plants—made their debut on the evolutionary stage. Angiosperm is an umbrella term that covers a wide range of plant types, from the prized cultivars in your garden to the unadorned weeds along the roadside. Although we don't think of trees such as oaks, maples, and willows as flowering plants, they are. In the spring their tiny, inconspicuous flowers produce lightweight pollen that is carried aloft by the spring breezes. Other deciduous trees, such as flowering dogwood, hawthorn, and black locust produce sweet-smelling flowers that lure insects to do the pollinating for them.

The samaras, or winged seeds, of all maple trees develop in pairs. Each member of the pair contains a maple seed. In the spring, look for samaras of silver maple, Norway maple, box elder, red maple, mountain maple, and striped maple. Samaras that develop on ashes, elms, yellow poplars, ailanthus, and basswood do not grow in pairs. Find some of these samaras and compare them with each other and with those from the maples.

1. Find a samara-producing tree. You will probably want to select a small tree for this activity.
2. Count the number of seeds per samara.
3. Count the number of samaras on a branch. (For our purposes, a branch is a large, secondary stem growing from the main trunk.)
4. Count the branches on your tree.
5. How many samaras are on the tree?
6. How many seeds are on the tree?
7. How many of this kind of tree are there in your neighborhood?
8. How many seeds (potential trees) of this type could be in your neighborhood?

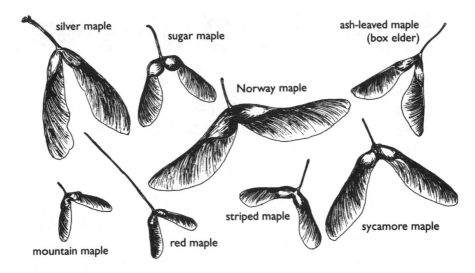

There is some variety in the appearance of samaras of different species of maple, but the basic design is the same. Each consists of a pair of winged seeds.

Examine Samaras

Samaras from different kinds of trees fall in different ways. Collect samaras from different kinds of trees. Samaras from sugar maples aren't available until fall, but silver maple samaras can be found in the spring.

1. To find out how they fall you could simply throw them into the air and watch them return to the ground. For a better look, throw them from a ladder or a second-story window. Are they rollers, tumblers, or undulators? Do the fruits of ash, maple, ailanthus, and yellow poplar all fall in the same way? Group them as to whether they roll, tumble, or undulate.

2. Measure the length and width of samaras from different trees. Does size influence the way they fall?

3. Remove the wings from some samaras in your collection and drop them from the same height as the winged samaras. How do the wings affect the fall of the fruit? How does a breeze affect the fall of a samara? What advantage is a samara to the tree species?

Study Galls

Galls are caused when an adult female insect lays its eggs on a particular part of a particular plant. Some insects lay their eggs on the surface of a plant part; others make a hole in the plant and lay their eggs inside. The exact nature of gall formation is not yet known. It is known that insects secrete growth-regulating chemicals called auxins. In response to the auxins secreted by an egg-laying female or by the larva that develops from the egg, the plant either produces new cells or enlarges some of the existing cells. The result is a gall unique to the insect that caused it.

Ball and elliptical galls are commonly found on goldenrod.

1. Find a field with goldenrod growing in it. Examine the goldenrod for galls on its stems. Is there more than one gall on each stem? What shapes are the galls? What percentage of the goldenrods you examined have galls? Which kind of gall occurs most frequently? Is it round or egg-shaped?

2. Look for tight bunches of leaves. Midges cause these galls called goldenrod bunch galls. Midges also cause raised black dots on the leaves. These are called blister galls. Galls also form on buds and flowers. Can you find any of these?

3. One researcher suggested that exit "doors" often face north and rarely face south. He reasoned that because the north-facing side of the gall received less sunlight, it would be moist and soft. The south-facing side of the gall would become dry and hard from the greater amount of sunlight. Since the moth larva could chew its "door" more easily on the softer, north-facing side, that's where the exit would be. Look for the tiny "door" on elliptical galls. Do the doors appear more frequently on the north-facing side or on the south-facing side of the gall?

4. The architecture inside galls is often very complex. To see some of this work you will need to open the galls. Some galls have a seam you can open with a fingernail or knife.

   Observe the inside of the gall. Is there one large chamber or are there several? Make some drawings to illustrate the interior design of the more elaborate galls you find. Are there any little larvae or grubs inside? How many can you find? Do you see any spiders living in the gall? Are there any other critters lodging inside? How many are there and what do they look like?

Examine Lichens

Perhaps the most basic and fascinating fact about lichens is that each lichen is composed of two very different kinds of plants. The lichen is a green or blue-green alga and a colorless fungus living together in a very special relationship.

The exact nature of the lichen partnership remains a puzzle. One theory is that the lichen union is beneficial to each organism. In this view, the alga provides food for itself and for the fungal partner through photosynthesis. In return, the fungus supplies chemicals that accelerate food production by the alga. The tough, spongy skin of the fungus also absorbs and stores water for use by both partners. This is called the *mutualistic theory.*

1. Lichens growing on tree trunks are often confused with fungi that also prefer this habitat. With your pocket knife, chip a piece of lichen and the bark that holds it.

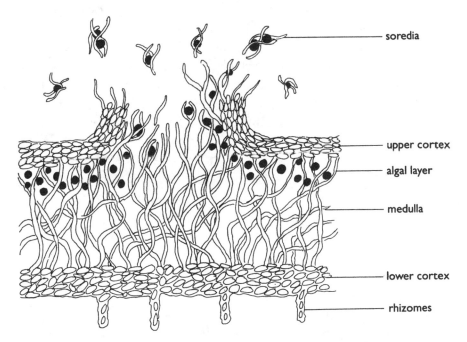

soredia

upper cortex

algal layer

medulla

lower cortex

rhizomes

Cross section of a lichen. In lichen reproduction, algal cells surrounded by soredia are released to drift away on wind currents.

Are the anchoring threads attached to the bark, or are the filaments growing through the bark? Is there a mass of cottonlike material on the underside of the bark? Lichens generally do not harm the tree. Some fungi are parasitic, however, and can damage the tree.

2. Lichen bodies are made of several layers. One of those layers contains green or blue-green algal cells held by fungal filaments. Cut across the lichen body as in the illustration. With a hand lens, look for the layers. What is the color of the cortex, or skin, of your lichen? Look for the green algal layer, the white medulla that contains white fungal threads, and the lower surface or cortex.

3. Find a tree with lichens growing on its bark. Draw chalk lines around the tree trunk about one foot above and one foot below chest height. The band you have made should be about two feet wide. Examine the lichens that are inside the band. Does there seem to be only one kind of lichen on the tree trunk, or are there different types?

4. With your compass, determine which portions of the tree are facing north, south, east, and west and mark them. Count the number of lichens in each section. Where are the greatest numbers of lichens? Is any portion of your band shaded throughout the day? How does this seem to affect the number and type of lichens growing on that part of the tree? Try a similar exploration to learn about the lichens that grow on rocks. What differences did you discover?

5. Find some lichens growing in an area that is easy for you to visit. With an 8½-by-11-inch piece of flexible transparent plastic, cover the lichens with the plastic and secure it with some tape. Using a permanent marker such as oil-based paint, draw the four corners of the plastic on the lichen foundation. You now have a reference point to use when you return to take measurements of lichen growth.

6. Lay the plastic sheet over the lichen you are studying. With a fine, felt-tipped pen, trace its outline onto the plastic sheet. Record on your plastic sheet the date of your tracing and the precise location of the lichen. When you return to the site at a future date, you can make another tracing of the same lichen by simply slipping your plastic sheet into the corners you made with the paint.

7. How much did the lichens grow over a summer, in a year, or in several years? Did they grow evenly around a central point or did one portion grow more than another? Describe the growth pattern. Find several lichens of the same type growing in different locations and repeat the steps. What was the average rate of growth for that type of lichen?

8. Make a photographic record of the lichens you find. A 35-mm camera with a macro lens for close-ups should work well. You might need a flash attachment if you are working in the dim light of a spruce-fir forest. Be sure to record the date you took the pictures, the location of each lichen, the type of foundation, and whether the lichen was wet or dry (color is sometimes altered by moisture).

Classify Vines

Vines come in a variety of sizes and shapes. You will find them growing on trees, shrubs, and bushes in backyards, parks, and schoolyards. They climb up buildings and telephone poles. You may even find an old house or barn covered by a blanket of vines. Look for vines at the woodland-field border where grasses, weeds, vines, and shrubs battle for dominance.

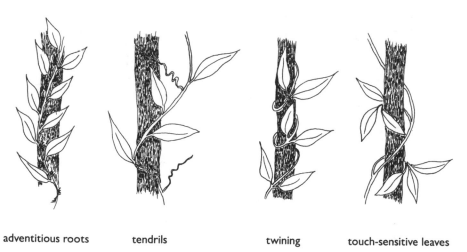

adventitious roots   tendrils   twining   touch-sensitive leaves

Vines use specific climbing strategies to reach sunlight.

1. Find a vine that twines up a vertical support. Invent a way to determine if the vine will continue to twine if the support is placed in a horizontal position.

2. Find a vine that uses tendrils to climb. Locate a tendril that is not wrapped around a support. Stroke one side of the tendril very gently with the point of a pencil. What happens and how long does it take? Examine several other kinds of vines that produce tendrils. Do the tendrils on these vines respond to touch in the same way?

3. Examine the tendrils of Boston ivy or English ivy. How many disks grow from each tendril? What do the disks look like? Can you pull them off the wall easily? On what kind of surfaces do you find them growing? Wood? Concrete? Brick? Smooth or rough?

4. Find the attachment disks of Virginia creeper. Describe the tendrils that are not attached to some object. What color are they? How big are they? What happens to the tendrils after they have become attached to a support? What color are the tendrils that are already in place on a support? Are they straight or twisted? Compare the tendrils and the disks of an older part of the vine with that of the younger portion. What do you notice?

5. Find a spring scale, like that used in fishing to weigh the catch. Attach one end of a string to the scale and the other end to a tendril. You can use some tape to secure the string to the tendril. How much force is required to pull the disk away from the surface where it was attached? Try this with other disk-attached vines, such as Boston ivy and English ivy.

Compare Millipedes and Centipedes

Plant-eating millipedes and meat-eating centipedes are among the many creatures you'll find as you go about your springtime forays. Look beneath decaying logs, leaf litter, and assorted rocks, and you will see these insects scurry for cover. Superficially similar, these two very different members of the myriapod (many-legged) group are often confused with one another.

You will need to trap a few centipedes and millipedes for these observations, but don't collect them until you're ready to use them. Centipedes have been known to eat each other when no other food is available, so put each in its own container. Millipedes can be put together in a container. Keep a piece of moist paper towel in with your creatures.

1. Centipedes are very active and often won't keep still long enough for you to observe them closely. Exposure to cold slows them down, so put your centipedes (in their container) into the refrigerator. Leave them there for a few hours.

2. In the meantime capture a millipede. To get a good look at its head, gently grasp it with pair of tweezers. Use a hand lens for a better look.

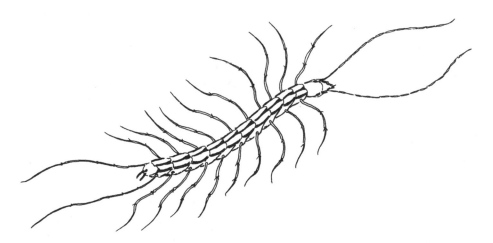

Centipedes, like this house centipede (class Chilopoda), have flexible exoskeletons that allow them to squeeze into tight spaces in search of food.

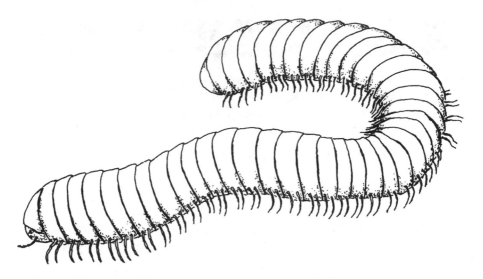

Millipedes (class Diplopoda) have hard, calcium-rich exoskeletons to protect themselves from predators.

3. Remove the centipede from the cold. Compare it with the millipede. What are the similarities and differences? Begin with the head, antennae, legs on each segment, length of legs, leg movements, and body shape. Watch a centipede move in the leaf litter or in a flat container. Compare it with the movement of a millipede.
4. Put a millipede on a three-foot-square piece of drawing paper. As it begins to explore, trace its path with a magic marker. Is its path straight, curved, or a squiggle? Put the millipede back at the starting point. Does it follow the same path this time?
5. Arrange the paper so that only half is in the sun. Does the millipede travel away from the sun or toward it? Try this a few more times. Can you find a pattern to the millipede's movements?
6. Put the millipede in a shoe box. Where does the millipede spend most of its time? In the middle of the box or crawling along the edge?
7. Collect a few millipedes. Put them, one at a time, on a large open space, such as the floor. What is the average distance your millipedes will crawl in one minute? Try this exploration with centipedes. You will want to contain them inside barriers, so that they don't disappear.

8. Find out what the centipede does when no tight spaces are available. Get a deep-sided container, such as a baking pan. Put about an inch of soil in it. Then put a centipede in the center of the container. What does the centipede do in the absence of snug hiding places? Where does it go? How long does it spend in each spot? Do other centipedes respond the same way?

9. Remove the centipede and add some leaf litter and several pieces of tree bark to the container. Put the centipede back into the center of the container. What does it do now? Do other centipedes respond in a similar way? Try the same investigation with millipedes. Do they seek out snug spaces in the same way that centipedes do?

10. Put some soil in the baking pan. Divide the pan in half with a waterproof barrier, such as a ruler, that is not higher than the soil surface. Moisten one half of the soil. Put a millipede on the dry side. What happens? How long does the millipede take to act?

   Try the same exercise with a centipede. Does it react in the same way as the millipede? On which side of the pan do the myriapods spend most of their time?

   Note: If you want to observe both millipedes and centipedes at the same time, put them in separate pans. A hungry centipede that is unable to find other food may make a meal of the lumbering millipede.

Study Earthworms

Since earthworms thrive on a diet of organic material, one of the best places to find them is in a well-tended garden. Earthworms cannot survive the ultraviolet rays of the sun, so they have evolved a simple behavioral strategy that reduces their risk of exposure—they generally come aboveground only at night. Cover the lens of a flashlight with a piece of red cellophane because a bright, white light signals them to seek shelter. With a dim, red light you'll be able to see them without them seeing you.

You also can find earthworms in the daytime just by digging in your own garden. A shovelful of rich soil will often yield a generous supply of earthworms. Also look for them under leaf litter and decaying logs.

When you have found some worms, put them into a large flat pan with a thin layer of soil, and begin your investigation simply by observing what they do. Remember an earthworm cannot hurt you, but you can injure it if you don't handle it gently.

1. Put an additional two or three inches of soil into your container. Put a worm on top of the soil. How long does it take the worm to burrow out of sight? Try this several times. What is the least amount of time it took a worm to disappear? The most time? The average time? Is the burrowing speed of the worms related to their length? Do larger worms burrow faster than smaller worms?

2. Put your earthworm on a moist paper towel. With a blunt pencil gently tap various parts of the earthworm body. Which part made the earthworm squiggle the most when you touched it, the head, tail, or middle? Gently poke the clitellum (the wide band around the worm's center). How does the worm respond? Try these tests with some other earthworms. Do they respond in a similar way? Can you make any generalizations about the sensitivity of the earthworm body to touch?

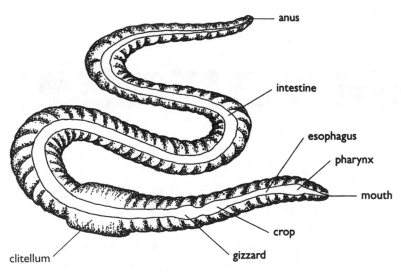

Anatomy of an earthworm

3. How do earthworms respond to light? To answer this question you will need two empty coffee cans. You will also need a dark cloth to cover one coffee can and transparent plastic wrap for the other. Put soil in the cans, add a few earthworms to each, and cover them. Check occasionally to find out which worms dug under first.

Make a Turtle Racetrack

Turtles are curious creatures. Their solitary nature has long intrigued and mystified us, but though they have been the subject of much interest and speculation, surprisingly little is known about how they make their living. Turtles, snakes, and other reptiles are grouped with amphibians in a branch of zoology called herpetology. The term is derived from the Greek word *herpeton*, which means "crawling things."

Even though reptiles and amphibians are very different kinds of creatures, early naturalists thought the two groups of animals were more closely related than they really are. The practice of grouping them together has historical roots and persists today. There is some confusion over the terms tortoise, terrapin, and turtle. Tortoises are essentially

Painted turtle (Chrysemys picta), *6 to 8 inches*

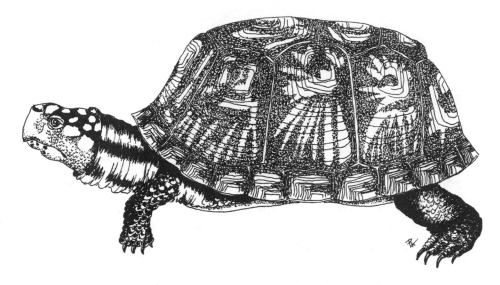

Eastern box turtle (Terrapene carolina), *4 to 6 inches*

creatures of the land, while terrapins live in the water. The term turtle is generally appropriate for all.

Some turtles move much faster than others. Stage a turtle race with some of your friends and their turtles. Most turtles you might find would be suitable, but do not use snapping turtles, which will bite if not handled properly.

1. To set up your racetrack, make a circle six feet in diameter.

2. Then make another circle around the first with a diameter of twelve feet.

3. In the center of the first circle, place a bull's-eye. This will be the starting place for the race, so be sure it is large enough to accommodate all the competing turtles.

4. You will need a timekeeper with a stopwatch, whose job it will be to call the start of the race and who will call the end when the first turtle crosses over the outside circle.

5. Predict which turtle will move the fastest and which the slowest. On what did you base your predictions? The turtles' overall size? The way the plastrons fit the limbs? Do the legs seem to have much freedom of movement, or does the lower shell fit snugly around the turtle's legs?

6. When you have made your predictions, put the turtles on the bull's-eye and let the race begin.

7. If no one else in the neighborhood has a turtle, you can still have a race in which your turtle competes against itself. It can challenge its own records. With the help of a stopwatch and a tape measure, you can find out how fast your turtle moves.

Test a Turtle's Sense of Smell

To find out if turtles can smell, try a little investigation.

1. Hang two bags, one containing some chopped meat and another filled with sand, in a box with your turtle. Which of the two bags attracts the turtle?

2. Repeat the investigation on several different occasions, hanging the bags in different locations in the turtle box. What happens each time? Does the turtle peck at the bag containing the meat while ignoring the bag containing the sand? What generalizations can you make about turtles and their ability to smell, based on their behavior?

Observe Turtles and Temperature Changes

The internal temperature and the metabolic rate of turtles and other reptiles are controlled by the temperature of the air around them. The colder the air becomes, the less active the turtles will be.

1. During the early spring, visit a local pond and measure the temperature of the air and that of the water near the surface and at the bottom of the pond (attach a thermometer to a stick long enough to reach the bottom of the pond). Record the readings.

2. Return to your pond regularly as the temperature increases through April. On what date do you see your first turtle? What was the temperature of the pond and of the air that day?

Turn Turtles

Occasionally a turtle will need to climb over a log or some other obstacle in its path, or it may tumble down a sandy bank or a pile of rocks. When this happens, the turtle may flip over and land upside down. This is a potentially dangerous situation for the turtle. Lying upside down in the sun can be fatal if the turtle cannot right itself quickly.

1. To find out how a turtle rights itself, gently put it on its back and watch its behavior. Does it use its head or legs in the process? How does the turtle shell help or hinder this process?

2. Record what the turtle does with its head, neck, tail, and legs. How long does it take the turtle to turn itself right side up? Most can right themselves after a few tries. What kinds of turtles do you think have the most difficulty turning themselves right side up? Do you think the length of the legs might be a factor? What part does the design of the shell play?

Observe Chipmunks

You can find the eastern chipmunk (*Tamias striatus*) as easily in wooded urban parks as you can in a forest. They are common visitors to campsites where they can get a friendly handout. Listen to them scamper in the woodland underbrush. In areas with enough trees and food you can even find their nests in abandoned buildings.

The smallest chipmunk in North America is the least chipmunk (*Eutamias minimus*). Look for them at the forest's edge or in second-growth areas that have been timbered or burned. Chipmunks also live in the alpine tundra.

Yellow-pine chipmunks (*Eutamias amoenus*) prefer high altitudes within their range, but they can also be found in grassy valleys. They like areas covered by low shrubs. Because of their remote habitat, they don't have much contact with people. But they won't turn down an offer of sunflower seeds from a friendly wilderness camper.

All chipmunk species display similar characteristics, such as the stripes that allow them to hide effectively on the forest floor.

Unlike other chipmunks, Townsend chipmunks (*Eutamias townsendii*) prefer coastal regions within their west coast range. It's not unusual to find them on timber-studded beaches and in the ferny underbrush of coastal forests.

1. Compared with squirrels, chipmunks don't have a good sense of smell. Their ears, however, are superb instruments for picking up sounds. Toss a peanut on the ground near a chipmunk. How does it find the nut? Can the chipmunk find it as easily if you toss it farther away?

2. Chipmunks display a wide range of behaviors. Below is a description of some behaviors and their labels.

    If the chipmunk is sitting with its front paws on ground and its back straight, it is alert. If its body is flat on the ground and its back is arched, the chipmunk is frozen. If a chipmunk is standing upright with its back straight and paws not clasped, it is in the duckpin position. When the tail is loosely coiled or on the ground, it is relaxed. When held upright, it is in alarm position.

3. Chipmunks will gather as many nuts as they can find, even when their stores are well stocked. Watch as a chipmunk gathers nuts.

How many does it put in its pouches? What types of food do chipmunks seem to prefer? On the ground, place a variety of nuts, such as hazelnuts, almonds, hickories, and acorns from white oaks. Which do they eat? Offer other foods, such as blueberries, strawberries, and orange slices. Does the chipmunk eat these?

4. During fall foraging and spring mating chipmunks are very active, so you might be able to find a chipmunk burrow. Watch the chipmunks that enter and leave the burrow.

   Are there any distinctive behaviors or markings on the chipmunk that help you to distinguish them from each other? A scar on its ear or on its shoulder? A tattered tail? Is there a behavior that's unique to a particular chipmunk?

5. Watch a chipmunk as it goes off to find some food. How long did it take the chipmunk to return? Does it follow the same path back to the burrow each time, or does it make new paths? Does the path follow a straight line? What happens if you put an obstacle, such as a row of small rocks, across the path?

6. You'll have to be up early to find out what a chipmunk does first thing in the morning. At what time did the chipmunk first appear? Did it first poke its nose out of the burrow and look around, or did it emerge all the way? What did it do when it came out?

7. Observe chipmunks grooming. Because mites and fleas are often problems, chipmunks frequently take dust baths to remove bugs and excess oil from their fur. Observe a dust bath.

8. One song chipmunks sing is a high-pitched chip, which they often repeat for an extended period of time. What is the longest time you hear them sing that song? Another sound chipmunks make is a combination of a chip followed by a trill. It is usually sung after danger has passed. Listen for it. A third sound is a soft, low-pitched, clucking sound. Chipmunks are good ventriloquists, so it may be difficult to find the source of the sounds.

Observe Gray Squirrels

Gray squirrels belong to an order of mammals called rodents. The order contains beavers, chipmunks, and voles, as well as the less popular rats and mice. The squirrel family includes the burrowing ground squirrels, such as prairie dogs, thirteen-lined ground squirrels, arctic ground squirrels, eastern chipmunks, and groundhogs (woodchucks), as well as the flying squirrels and the tree squirrels. Members of the tree squirrel group are the eastern gray squirrel (*Sciurus carolinensis*), the western gray squirrel (*S. griseus*), the eastern fox squirrel (*S. niger*), and the red squirrel (*Tamiasciurus hudsonicus*), sometimes called the spruce squirrel.

You can find squirrels around your house, in parks, and most everywhere that food and shelter is available to them. Observe a squirrel from a distance to learn more about it.

1. How long is the squirrel's tail? Is it longer or shorter than the squirrel body, or the same? How does a squirrel use its tail as it leaps from tree to tree? As the squirrel runs along a fence or stone wall, does it hold its tail up in the air or move it from side to side? Does the squirrel hold its tail directly behind its body during these maneuvers? Since squirrels can move quickly (up to fifteen miles per hour), you will want to check your observations by watching more than one squirrel.

2. Squirrels take special care of their tails. Watch the squirrel groom its tail. How long does it take? Does the squirrel follow any particular pattern, or is the cleaning a haphazard process?

3. Squirrels are very vocal: they growl, gurgle, purr, buzz, and chatter. As you walk in the woods or in a wooded park, listen for squirrel noises. Squirrel sounds are often accompanied by tail waving or tail flicking. Can you infer from these behaviors what the sounds mean? Consider danger, anger, and excitement.

4. In March, when the sap in the trees begins to flow, look for squirrels chewing on sap icicles that formed during the night. They love the sweet taste of sap, especially from sugar maples. Look for squirrels eating the tender young leaves of oaks and maples, and the blossoms of shagbark hickories and elms.

Squirrrels nest in tree holes for the winter when they can find them. They often line them with leaves or other soft material for warmth.

5. A squirrel's winter home is usually the dry hollow of an abandoned woodpecker hole. Look for these nests especially in oak or beech trees. The nest is lined with grass, moss, and shredded leaves. Nests in tree hollows are used for breeding and raising the first litter of three or four young squirrels. Do the squirrels make their nests in the same trees during successive winters? Do the squirrels leave and return to the nest by way of the same path? Are the paths always along the ground, or are some in the treetops? Does more than one squirrel use a trail? Make a map showing the trails of the different squirrels that live in the nest.

6. Cats and squirrels can both climb trees. But have you ever seen a squirrel back down a tree trunk? Squirrels have a neat adaptation that makes coming down as easy as going up. Can you discover it? A squirrel sensing danger on its way down the tree trunk will freeze. This is a good time to look at its paws.

7. Squirrels are well adapted for life in the trees. They have sharp claws for climbing and hanging, and sturdy, muscular hind legs for jumping. One squirrel-leaping record is an amazing sixty feet. Watch several squirrels as they leap from place to place. Estimate the average distance your squirrels can jump.

8. How close can you get to a squirrel before it scampers away? Does it make a difference from which direction you approach the squirrel? Try approaching several squirrels from different directions. What did you find out? Do urban squirrels allow you to get closer to them than woodland squirrels?

9. How do squirrels react when approached by other squirrels? Do they fight or chase? Do they ignore each other? How close will one squirrel allow another to approach before reacting?

Explore Beaver Dam Construction

Like most mammals that live in the wild, beavers are active at night, when they are less likely to be spotted by predators. Their preference for working in the diminishing evening light means that most people have not had an opportunity to observe them building their dams and lodges. Beavers (*Castor canandensis*) belong to a subgroup of mammals called rodents or Rodentia, from the Latin for "to gnaw," along with muskrats, minks, and river otters. The activities presented here encourage you to look at how beavers do their work and get a peek at the family life of these affectionate rodents.

When beavers move into a new area that lacks a pond, they construct a dam across a stream or river to restrict the flow of water and create a pond upstream of the dam. After beavers have selected a site for the dam, they begin felling trees. When a tree is down, the beaver trims off large branches, drags the log to the stream, and guides it to the dam site.

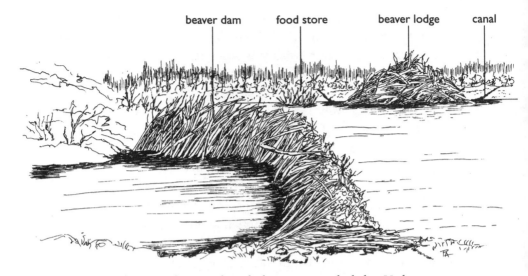

The beaver dam provides a pond in which to construct the lodge. Underwater tunnels lead to the living chamber. Branches stored nearby provide winter food. Canals help the beaver move logs to the building site.

Beavers lay the first logs side by side and jam them into the mud, with the butt ends facing downstream. In this position, the remaining branches catch debris and mud floating downstream, adding to the width of the dam. On this foundation, beavers pile anything they can find, such as sticks, stones, and wood chips, onto the upstream side of the dam. The downstream side of the dam is made primarily of sticks and branches. The beavers then fill the spaces between the upstream materials with mud and vegetation.

1. Explore ponds near your home, looking for beaver dams. If you find such a dam, look at the materials the beavers used.
2. Write the materials you observe in your notebook. Do you see evidence of human discards, such as automobile or bicycle tires, lumber, plastic, bottles, or cans? How long is the dam? How high above the water level of the pond is it? How high is it above the downstream side? How wide is the crest? Does the dam cross the stream in a straight line or does it zigzag? Can you find any evidence that the crest of the dam has been used as a bridge by animals such as muskrats or raccoons?

3. Examining a dam that is broken will give you a better appreciation for the skills required for building. If you come across such a dam, take some time to study its design. Make a drawing or photograph it for your field notebook. Can you identify some of the building materials the beavers used?

4. Beavers often build canals to help them move logs to a construction site. The canals also offer the beaver protection from land-based predators. The canals may be two feet wide and two feet deep. Do you see any canals leading to the beaver pond?

Observe Beavers

1. Beavers have blunt heads and small eyes and ears. With a stout body and short legs, it's impossible for the beaver to run quickly. Some say that beavers waddle. Do you agree? A pair of binoculars will help you get a better look at them. They are graceful and swift underwater, but this is not so easy to observe.

2. Beaver fur is chestnut to dark brown, but in the northern part of their range, it's almost black. The coat is designed to keep the beaver dry and warm, even though the beaver spends a great deal of time in the water. Beneath the long, coarse guard hairs lies an undercoat of shorter, finer fur of a lighter color than the guard hairs. This underfur is thickest on the beaver's back and gives the coat its softness and resistance to wetness. If you have a dog that has these two types of hair, you can easily examine the differences between the guard hairs and the soft fur of the undercoat. To see how well the undercoat works at keeping the animal dry, give the dog a bath. The addition of soap to the bath water helps get the undercoat wet.

3. The two inside toes of each foot of the beaver are equipped with specialized claws that serve as combs. Beavers comb their fur, dislodge parasites, and waterproof their fur with oil from their anal glands. In the wild, you won't be able to see these "combs," but you may be able to observe the grooming act. If you do, take a series of

photographs to show the process. Is there an order to it? What part of the body does the beaver groom first? What part is groomed last?

4. If you shine a flashlight at the eyes of a dog, they glow like burning coals. This does not occur with beavers. The eyes of dogs, like raccoons, have a reflective membrane called the *tapetum lucidum,* which lets them make the most use of available light, although the images are less clear. When you see these animals' eyes glow red in the beam of headlights or a flashlight, this is called eye shine and is the result of the light reflecting off the tapetum lucidum. If you shine a flashlight beam at beavers' eyes, they do not glow, as they lack the light-gathering membrane of many other nocturnal creatures. They see in the dark much as we do—not terribly well.

There is some speculation about the reason for this. Records of early observations indicate that the beaver was once quite active during some part of the day, and it was referred to as a diurnal animal. Some scientists think their nocturnal behavior is a fairly recent response to the species' survival being threatened by trappers.

3

IN THE GARDEN

Watch a Flower Pistil
Develop into a Fruit

The corolla of a standard backyard blossom is composed of five separate petals. Its hardly visible calyx is divided into five sepals, and there are five stamens (in the drawing, one lies behind the pistil). Moreover, our standard blossom's pistil possesses a roundish ovary, a short style, and a bi-lobed stigma.

The parts of a flower's anatomy and its uses are as follows:

Pedicel: the stem of an individual blossom

Calyx: the usually green, cuplike part of the flower below the corolla

Sepal: a lobe or division of the calyx

Corolla: usually the bright, pretty part of a blossom located immediately above the calyx

Petal: a lobe or division of the corolla

Stamen: the male part of a flower, composed of the anther and filament

Anther: the upper part of a stamen; produces pollen

65

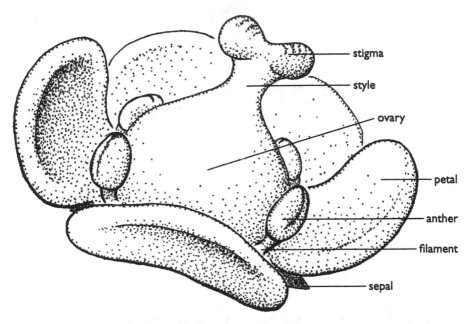

The "standard" backyard blossom possesses average traits: five identical sepals, petals, and stamens, and a plump ovary with a short style, beneath a shallowly lobed stigma.

Filament: the stalk of a stamen, supporting the anther

Pistil: the female part of the flower, composed of the stigma, style, and ovary

Stigma: the pistil's summit, where pollen grains germinate

Style: the part of the pistil connecting the stigma with the ovary

Ovary: the swollen, basal portion of a pistil; ovaries eventually develop into fruits

Ovules: the egglike items inside an ovary that, once fertilized, develop into seeds

1. Find a newly opened flower; bean or pea plants make good candidates. Tie a small ribbon or other marker below or near the blossom so that later you can easily find it.
2. Observe this blossom from day to day and notice how the pistil changes. As the pistil enlarges into a fruit, what happens to the stamens and corolla? Do the stigma and style enlarge as the ovary grows?

Force Daffodils

Daffodils are among the best plants to force, or "trick," into flowering much earlier than they would if left alone. Hyacinths, tulips, and crocuses also are easily forced. Forcing enables us to have cheery, living bouquets on our window sills while it's still snowy outside.

1. In the fall, around October 1, dig up some daffodil bulbs, or buy some. The larger, firmer, and more perfectly formed they are, the better. Some daffodil varieties force better than others. For early results, some good varieties include Rembrandt, Orange Queen, Golden Harvest, Forerunner, and February Gold.

2. Fill the pot with potting soil to about half an inch below the pot's rim. Water thoroughly. Throughout the winter, keep the soil moist, but not waterlogged.

3. Bury the bulbs with their necks slightly protruding above the potting soil. It's important for the bulbs to experience winter's cold and moistness, but they should not freeze. One way to provide this environment is to sink the pots in the ground or place them in a cold frame, and then bury them beneath six inches or more of mulch. Another way is to store the pots in a closet, attic, or attached garage, where temperatures never dip below freezing or rise above 50 °F; these will need to be watched closely, to guard against the potting soil drying out.

4. The bulbs should remain in this cool, moist environment for at least six to ten weeks. This is an important time for the plants because this is when the bulbs sprout their roots. Bulbs placed in the cool, moist environment on October 1 can be brought inside the warm house in late November for a flowering date of Christmas, or early January, depending on the variety chosen, house temperature, bulb health, and amount of light. House temperatures between 65 and 75 °F are best; the colder the temperature, the slower the blooms develop. Also, the closer to spring one brings the bulbs indoors, the more quickly the blooms appear.

5. If the blossoming daffodil's room temperature stays around 70 °F and is fairly moist, the blossoms may stay pretty for a couple of weeks. Once the blossoms fade, snip off the flower stems and set

the pots somewhere cool and moist, so that in the spring the bulbs can be planted. During next year's spring, the bulbs may issue only leaves and no flowers, but by the second spring the bulbs should have recuperated, and will probably blossom. Bulbs don't force well a second time.

Grow Sprouts in a Jar

Inside most kinds of seeds found in our gardens and flower beds, there are two general areas. First, there is a relatively large zone of whitish, unstructured, starchy or oily materials; this is food for the future germinating seedling. When the embryo first begins growing, extending its shoot up through the sunless soil, it will not be able to manufacture its own food the way mature green plants do, because that requires sunlight. At this critical time, it will tap the energy stored in this high-calorie "seed food."

When a bean, or nearly any of our common garden plants except corn and other monocots, first emerges from the soil, two green, thick, kidney-shaped leaflike things first appear, and then the stem with regular-shaped and normal-textured leaves emerges from between the two leaflike things. Those first two leaflike things are called the cotyledons.

1. Various kinds of beans or seeds for sprouting can be purchased at a health food store. They should be fairly new ones meant for sprouting, or else they may be dead or weak and will not germinate properly. Don't use beans meant to be sown; these may be treated with toxic fungicides and insecticides.

2. Cut a circular nylon or cheesecloth cover for the jar's mouth, about six inches across. Make sure the jar and covering are clean.

3. Pour some beans or seeds into the jar. A surprisingly small amount goes a long way—about one and a half cups of large beans such as soy, one cup of smaller mung beans, or a half cup of tiny alfalfa seeds will do.

4. Stretch the covering across the jar's mouth so that it is taut, and secure it with the rubber band. The rubber band should be tight

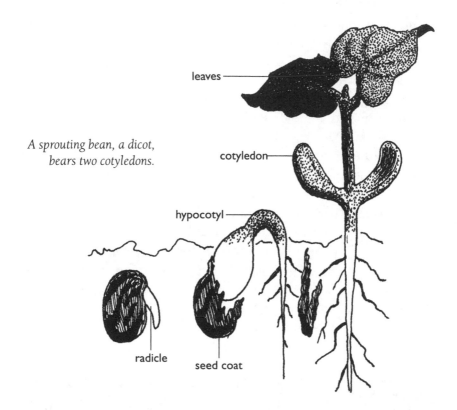

A sprouting bean, a dicot, bears two cotyledons.

leaves

cotyledon

hypocotyl

radicle

seed coat

enough to hold the covering on when the sprouts are being washed.

5. Wash the beans by filling the jar one-quarter full with tap water, swirling, then pouring off the excess water through the nylon or cheesecloth.

6. Fill the jar two-thirds full of water, and soak the seeds. Soak soybeans overnight. Smaller mung and alfalfa seeds can be ready in about six hours, but soaking overnight won't hurt.

7. After soaking, pour out all the water. If using small seeds, which tend to clump together, roll the jar so that the seeds will adhere to the jar's wet inner surface instead of clumping; the idea is to make free air available to all seeds. Soybeans are so big that air circulates around them as they lie on the jar's bottom.

8. Store the jar in its sprouting place. No light is needed; anyplace will do, even inside a cabinet, as long as it's neither too hot (fungi will

grow) or too cold (germination slows down). A corner shelf in the laundry room is good.

9. Wash the beans each morning and night by running tap water into the jar, sloshing the contents around, and pouring out the liquid, repeating this procedure three or four times.

10. Alfalfa sprouts are ready for harvesting once they reach one to two inches long. Mung sprouts should be two to three inches, and soybean sprouts about one-and-three-quarters inches. When the sprouts are big enough, spread them on a tray and place them in the sunlight for half an hour or so; on cloudy days, let them stay out longer. This activates photosensitive enzymes, which make the sprouts more nutritious. Also, the chlorophyll thus produced will add a green coloration, making them look more appetizing.

11. Eat your sprouts! Don't just shyly sprinkle a few onto salads, in soups, or in sandwiches—use them by the handfuls. Nothing is as good as a crunchy heap of alfalfa sprouts on whole-grain bread, maybe smeared with a little salad dressing.

Plant Seeds in a Cup

1. Prepare a sterile seed-starting soil mixture. Regular garden soil is undesirable because it contains disease organisms that can kill sprouting seeds. Mix one part store-bought peat moss with two parts potting soil, or mix equal parts of peat moss and vermiculite. Moisten this mixture, and add a little fertilizer.

2. Now fill a cup equipped with a drainage hole to about half an inch from the rim.

3. Atop the soil mixture, place one to three seeds of a garden plant of your choice. If you have seeds packaged for the current year and proper, sterile soil mixture, the seeds will almost invariably sprout. If you want insurance, however, plant two or three seeds, then later snip down the less vigorous.

4. Cover the seeds with soil mixture. As a general rule, the appropriate depth is usually three to four times the seed's diameter. (This depth is generally given on the seed packet.) Firm down the soil

with a couple of gentle pats, making sure that the seeds make good contact with the moist mixture.

5. Place the cup inside a sealed plastic bag. At this point, the soil mixture should be moist but not so wet that water is running out the hole. Thus covered, the cup will require no further watering until the seedling is well established.

6. Once the seedling has sprouted and is well established, remove the bag, and begin occasional sprinkling with fertilizer-enriched water. Sprinkle once a day, just enough to keep the soil mixture moist and spongy. The sterile soil is low in nutrients, so it is important to use fertilizer. A balanced liquid fertilizer with an N–P–K (nitrogen, phosphorus, and potassium) analysis of 15–30–15 is fine.

Test for Sunlight-Produced Carbohydrate

Through photosynthesis, earth's green plants capture sunlight energy by bonding together carbon, hydrogen, and oxygen atoms from carbon dioxide and water to form a carbohydrate. Scientifically, a carbohydrate can be defined as molecules composed of carbon, hydrogen, and oxygen. As we perceive it, a carbohydrate is a white, starchy material. The starchy part of the stored food found in seeds is mostly carbohydrate.

In a way, plants storing energy in photosynthesized carbohydrates and then using that energy later is like a person lifting a rock onto a table, and then later pushing the rock off the table to crack a nut on the floor. Once the rock is on the table, it has potential energy. That abstract energy has been transferred into the rock from the person as he or she used energy to lift the rock. Once the rock is pushed off the table, its potential energy is used in the act of smashing the nut.

1. The day before you do this experiment, locate a broad leaf that remains in sunlight all day long and that you can clip off at the end of this experiment. A fast-growing leaf of a bean plant would be perfect. A fast-growing leaf is a young leaf about two-thirds grown, rapidly expanding in size. Mark the leaf so that you can find it later.

2. Fold a sheet of stiff, black paper across the middle, with the fold parallel with the short sides. (The paper should be thick enough that sunlight will not penetrate, but not so thick that it cannot be easily folded.) In one half, cut a simple design, such as a circle, a diamond, or a star.

3. In the early morning before the sun comes up, sandwich your chosen leaf between the halves of the folded card so that the cutout design faces the sky. You want sunlight to be blocked from all parts of the leaf except for what passes through the cutout design. Secure the paper onto the leaf with paper clips or adhesive tape.

4. At day's end, remove the whole leaf. Inside the house, remove the folded paper.

5. In a small pan, pour about half an inch of rubbing alcohol. Drop the leaf into the pan.

6. On an electric stove, bring the alcohol to a boil. Use a lower heat than is needed for boiling water, because alcohol boils at a much lower temperature. The medium setting should be adequate. An electric stove is required because alcohol is flammable.

   Important: Don't heat the alcohol over an open flame or at too high a temperature, or you may cause a fire! An easygoing boil will do. If the boiling becomes too vigorous, lift the pan off the burner until the boiling calms down. Since odoriferous, eye-burning fumes rise off boiling alcohol, use the stove's ventilation hood.

7. Once the alcohol has become dark with chlorophyll boiled from the leaf and the leaf itself is much paler than before, remove the pan from the heat. Carefully remove the leaf with a pair of tongs and place it on a saucer.

8. Using a Q-tip or an eyedropper, apply iodine evenly over the leaf's surface. If the experiment is a success, a dark design matching the pattern cut into the paper should appear on the blanched leaf.

9. Keeping in mind that iodine stains carbohydrate a very dark purple color, reflect on the meaning of the dark purple pattern.

10. The experiment had you affix the paper to the leaf in the early morning because at that time stored carbohydrate in leaves is at a low point, some having been consumed as the leaf respired during

the night, and some having been transported to the plant's food-storage areas. Late in the afternoon of a sunny day, those parts of the leaf that have received sunlight will contain a maximum amount of carbohydrate because it will have been photosynthesized by the leaf over the course of the day.

Analyze Apples

A ripe apple's sweetness reveals the presence of sugars. So where do the sugars come from? As an apple ripens, its long carbohydrate molecules break down to much shorter ones, the shortest of which are the simple sugars known as sucrose (table sugar) and fructose. The following activity illustrates how different carbohydrates affect an apple's taste.

1. Slice open an unripe apple, and take a small bite of it. Your tongue should quickly inform you that there's very little apple taste there. In fact, the apple is so sour that it may sting your tongue. This sourness indicates that unripe apples are full of various kinds of acids.

2. Smell the unripe green apple. You should detect very little, if any, "apple" odor. This indicates that the acids present are not the kind that evaporate and waft into the nose; they are nonvolatile acids, such as malic and citric acids.

3. Nibble on the unripe apple's skin. Your lips should pucker a little. This is caused by tannic acid, famous for its pucker-causing quality.

4. Now go through the above steps with a ripe apple. You will find, of course, that the apple not only tastes like an apple, but also is sweet, smells fruity, and will not pucker the lips. Obviously, enormous chemical changes have taken place.

Grow a Colossal-Size Pumpkin

Raising your own vegetables can be an inexpensive and healthy alternative to buying them from the store. You will always get the freshest vegetables available, picking them from your garden moments before they are cooked and eaten. Depending on your family's preferences, you can grow as much or as little as you need of any vegetable. Directions on how to grow specific vegetable plants appear on seed packets, on flowerpot and seed-tray labels, and in gardening books. You can also visit your local library and thumb through gardening books to learn many fascinating facts about vegetables.

Nowadays a few people grow pumpkins for pies, but most gardeners seem to plant them just for the fun of watching the big, friendly looking fruits develop, and then having them on hand at Halloween.

1. In the spring, once the ground is thoroughly warm and all danger of frost is past, dig a hole about two feet across and two feet deep in a well-drained spot that receives sunlight the whole day.

2. Next to the hole, mix equal parts of well-digested compost or aged barnyard manure with the soil just removed from the hole. If you do not have compost or manure, mix about a pound of balanced fertilizer, such as a 10-10-10, with a bushel of soil. If the soil is very clayey, add enough sand or peat moss to make it loose and crumbly.

3. Shovel the soil mixture back into the hole. If you've enriched the soil with compost or manure, mound it into a hill about a foot high. If the soil is enriched with commercial fertilizer, make the mound about eight inches high, then add about three inches of loose, crumbly unfertilized soil atop that.

4. Plant three or four pumpkin seeds in the hill.

5. Once the plants bear three or four leaves, cut (don't pull) all plants except the biggest one.

6. After your remaining plant has produced three or four pumpkins, pick off all blossoms and all vine tips; there's no use having the plant waste energy on future pip-squeak pumpkins and wide-ranging vines.

If you follow these directions, you too can grow a humongous pumpkin.

7. When the pumpkins are about softball-size, grit your teeth and cut off all but the best one. Be delicate here; damaging the stem could wreck plumbing needed for a smooth, regular conduction of water and nutrients into the future giant.

8. Big pumpkins flatten as they grow. If you want a perfectly shaped one and you're willing to live dangerously (the danger being that you might damage the stem or leaves), every couple of weeks delicately shift the fruit's position.

9. Harvest the pumpkin when it seems to be finished growing. Don't remove the stem from the pumpkin; this causes the fruit to deteriorate. If you have a hard time getting the pumpkin unattached from its vine, use pruning shears or even a saw.

Fry Squash Blossoms to Eat

The word squash is of American Indian origin: In Algonquian, *askoot-asquash* means "eaten green." Today, various squashes are exceedingly important to isolated American Indian communities, especially in Latin America. In southern Mexico's markets, sometimes the large, orange squash flowers are sold as food.

1. Pick squash flowers just unfurling into open blossoms, and wash them. If the stamen filaments feel stiff, remove them.

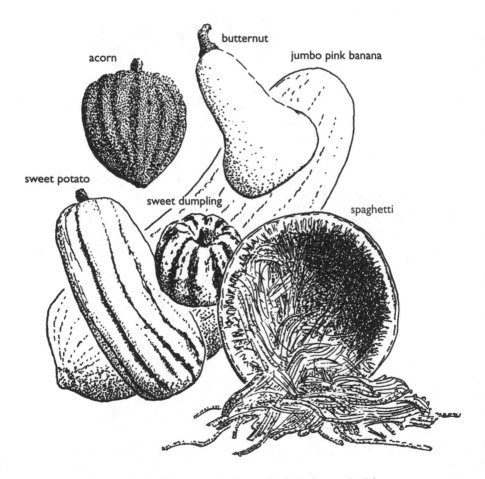

Squash come in a variety of shapes and colors, all of which provide delicious nourishment.

2. Oil a skillet and heat it up on medium. Some people deep-fry their flowers in a pool of very hot oil or grease; I prefer using just enough to keep things from sticking. A cooking spray like Pam works fine.

3. Mix the flour, salt, pepper, and egg into a bowl, then beat in enough water, milk, or buttermilk to form a loose batter of the consistency proper for pancakes.

4. Dip the blossoms into the batter, covering them entirely.

5. Fry until the batter is golden brown. If the batter begins burning on the outside but remains wet next to the flowers, turn the heat down. Once one side looks done, flip the blossom and fry the other side.

Grow Sweet Potato Slips

Sweet potatoes are propagated by slips—little green-stemmed sprouts with roots on them sprouted from sweet potatoes. These slips are available at garden centers and from seed catalogs. They can also be grown from store-bought sweet potatoes, as described in the following project, which is best timed for seven or eight weeks before spring's average last frost date.

1. Obtain as many sweet potatoes as you need for the number of plants you want. One large sweet potato should produce about six slips. Sweet potatoes I've purchased in supermarkets have worked fine, but sometimes sprout-retarding chemicals have been sprayed on them. If possible, buy them in garden supply shops; if not, wash them very well.

2. Half fill the tray with moist peat moss.

3. Slice the sweet potatoes lengthwise down the middle.

4. Place the sweet potato halves atop the moist peat moss, cut face down, and entirely cover with a shallow layer of peat moss.

5. Cover the whole tray with cellophane.

6. As soon as shoots appear, remove the cellophane and place the tray in a sunny window.

7. After the last frost date, you can snap off each slip with its white roots attached to it, and plant them outside. Sweet potato vines sprawl quite a bit, so give them plenty of room.

Grow a Very Productive, Super-Pampered Tomato Plant

Though American Indians from Mexico to Peru ate tomatoes long before Europeans arrived in the New World, it took a while for people in the Old World to convince themselves that tomatoes were edible. For a long time Europeans suspected that tomatoes were poisonous. There was some basis for this; tomatoes are members of the nightshade family, and some nightshades are poisonous, such as tobacco, belladonna, mandrake, and jimsonweed.

1. Acquire one or more tomato slips. Tomato stems are incredibly fragile, so by no means buy slips bound together with rubber bands or string; each plant should grow snugly in its own little container of soil. The best tomato slips are about eight inches tall. Look for plants with thick, solid stems, and scan each plant for diseases and insects.

Tomatoes are vines and need to be staked or grown inside a wire cage.

2. Plants that have always lived indoors but now must live outdoors should be toughened up slowly. Before planting the slips, harden them off by setting the plants outside in a shady place for two or three days. If at any time the night temperatures are forecasted to reach below 40°F, bring the plants in overnight. For the next two or three days, keep the plants in a spot receiving three to four hours of daily sunshine. For two or three more days, place them where the sun hits daily for four or five hours.

3. If possible, transplant the slips late in the afternoon on a cloudy day. For each slip, dig a good-sized hole at least as deep and wide as the plant is tall. If you are setting more than one plant, place them two to three feet apart. If the soil that comes out is clayey, break it up and mix in two or three handfuls of compost or sand to make it crumbly. In the hole's bottom, place a heaping handful of well-digested compost, or a tablespoon of a balanced fertilizer, such as 5-10-10, mixed with two or three inches of soil. Do not over-fertilize, or you'll end up with lush foliage but few tomatoes.

4. Add a couple inches of nonenriched, loose soil atop that, and then place upon this the slip with its potting soil in place. Gingerly pull more loose soil around it. If you plan to later water by the bucket-ful, build a water-holding dike around the plant. To save on water, spread a thick mulch around the plant's base; don't mulch until the ground is warm, however.

5. For protection against cutworms, place a collar around the base of the plant; nearly anything will do, even a sheet of newspaper twisted and folded into a circle. It doesn't take much to discourage a cutworm.

6. Though it be painful to shear your beauties, once they're planted, pinch off the larger leaves, leaving just the top small ones; this reduces the set's trauma from transpiration.

7. Drive a sturdy stake about ten inches from each slip. Stakes should stand at least four feet high.

8. Soak the ground around the plants, and keep the soil moist over the next three or four days. Do what you can to protect the plants from cold and wind. You can keep plastic, gallon-size milk jugs with the bottoms cut out handy for covering the plants in blustery weather.

9. Tomato plants left unpruned produce shoots, or suckers, in leaf axils. These suckers produce more stems, leaves, flowers, and more suckers. Most gardeners, therefore, pull off unwanted suckers so that the plants will direct their energy into producing tomatoes rather than suckers. There's no fast rule for "suckering." A good technique is to let two or three side suckers grow to a comfortable height, and thereafter pinch off all growing tips.

10. As they grow, give your plants some kind of support. I tie my tomato plants to stakes and cages with strips cut from discarded nylon pantyhose. As we place the strips around the delicate stems, we spread them so that pressure is distributed over a large surface area; by no means should slender string or wire be used. Staked and caged tomatoes take up less space than sprawling ones, produce cleaner tomatoes with less rotting, have fewer slug problems, and are easier to pick. Erect plants will dry out more quickly, however, as the soil at the base of the plants is exposed, and thus they should be well mulched, or watered frequently.

11. Tomato plants can stand a tiny frost, but not much. On the autumn afternoon before the first predicted frost, I pick all immature tomatoes that are at least two-thirds of their mature size; most of them will ripen eventually. If you treat them gently and keep them in a cool, dry place, you can enjoy ripe tomatoes from the garden on Thanksgiving and, with a little luck, even at Christmas!

Make a Rainbow Bouquet

A weed is just a plant living where somebody, for some reason, doesn't want it. When looked at very closely—into their blossoms, underneath their leaves—weeds are truly as interesting and beautiful as a zinnia. Weeds in a garden contribute diversity, and diverse systems in nature are more productive, more sustainable, and much more interesting than simple ones.

Take a close look at a wild carrot's flowers. The snow-white, lacy affair known as Queen Anne's lace is actually a cluster of tiny flowers called an inflorescence. Inside each inflorescence, the individual flow-

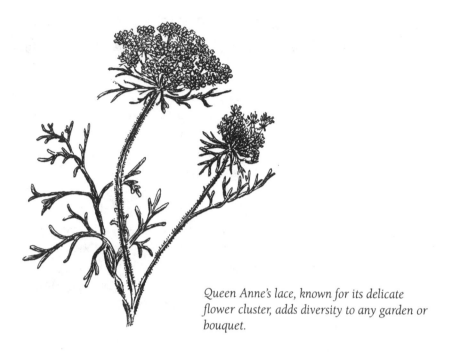

Queen Anne's lace, known for its delicate flower cluster, adds diversity to any garden or bouquet.

ers show surprising diversity. In the inflorescence's very center there's usually a single dark purple blossom. Flowers on the perimeter have longer pedicels, or flower stems, and enlarged corolla limbs. Once you've gotten to know a lot of plants, you'll realize that this is quite a special arrangement.

1. Snip off a few young, expanding Queen Anne's lace inflorescences.
2. In separate glasses of water, add a few drops of various hues of food coloring.
3. Place the stems of the inflorescences in the colored water, and watch as the white, lacy flowers take on pastel colors over a period of hours.
4. Use the colored inflorescences to make a rainbow bouquet.

Monitor Pupae

In complete metamorphosis, what emerges from an insect's egg is a larva. Larvae come in all shapes, colors, and sizes, and are often more colorful and better known than the adults. Many larvae are called caterpillars.

Larvae molt and grow through few to several instars (the stages between molts), sometimes changing in color, size, and other characteristics. At the end of the final instar stage, a decisive change occurs: instead of the larvae simply becoming larger, a pupa develops. Pupae are usually inactive and thus don't feed. Sometimes they are enclosed in a protective covering. If the covering is baglike and holds the insect inside, the covering is called a cocoon. If the covering is formed of the larva's exoskeleton, it's a puparium. In the special case of butterflies, whose pupae are often finely sculptured and sometimes brightly colored, the pupa is referred to as a chrysalis.

If you look around your garden long enough, usually you will be able to find various kinds of pupae. Being on hand when the adult finally emerges can be exciting.

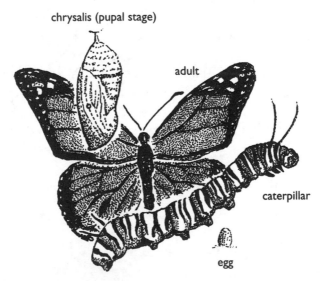

The monarch butterfly goes through four stages of metamorphosis.

1. Find one or more pupae; the best time to look is from late summer through early fall. Don't restrict your hunt to the garden—also look in surrounding trees and shrubbery. Look under leaves, deep inside vines and bushes, beneath loose tree bark, and among large wood chips. Don't search just once and then give up; as summer proceeds into fall, different species pupate.

2. Tie a brightly colored snippet of ribbon next to each resting pupa you discover.

3. In your notebook, sketch a map of the entire area searched, and mark the location of each pupa. The notebook will cue you to the pupa's general location, and the ribbon will show you exactly where it is. Note the date of discovery, and later the dates of any changes observed.

4. Sketch the pupae, drawing arrows to important features that might help in future identification. If you can identify either the pupa or the adult that later emerges, cross-reference your sketch with your page on that particular insect species.

5. Each day check on each pupa. If you're lucky, you may witness at least one emergence.

Create a Butterfly Garden

Butterfly watching has replaced butterfly collecting, and gardeners plant flowers that provide food for caterpillars and butterflies. Pins and mounting boards have yielded to binoculars and cameras, as live specimens delight observers more than preserved ones. Unlike birds, which often sing before the sun is above the horizon, butterflies don't stir unless the air is sufficiently warm, usually between about 9 A.M. and 6 P.M., depending on the time of year. Once you find a food source preferred by adult butterflies, all you have to do is wait and watch. A botanical garden or a local park with floral gardens is a good place to begin your adventure.

Pesticides and habitat destruction have made life extremely difficult for butterflies. By planting a garden with wildflowers and shrubs that attract butterflies, you will be helping them while getting an opportunity to enjoy their beauty. The garden does not need to be large.

1. You can add plants that will attract butterflies to an existing garden, or you can use patio containers or flower boxes.
2. To learn what plants attract butterflies in your area, visit public gardens, fields, meadows, and other sunny places during the flowering season. Field guides, botanical gardens, university botany and entomology departments, university extension services, and the people at local nurseries can help you find out more about plants butterflies love.
3. Some plants that attract butterflies are lilac, rhododendron, honeysuckle, butterfly bush, buttonbush, bee balm, daisies, dandelion, hawkweed, Queen Anne's lace, thistle, yarrow, aster, joe-pye weed, ironweed, and willow, plum, and cherry trees.

Build a Wire Fence–Contained Compost Heap

Composting is the process of turning biodegradable waste into a very useful material of a special kind. Something that is biodegradable is material that can be degraded, or decomposed, or turned back to the soil by regular biological processes such as rotting and decaying. In the backyard, biodegradable things are nearly always forms of organic matter. Organic matter is simply a matter that is or once was alive. All organic matter is biodegradable if toxic chemicals haven't been added.

In a properly functioning compost heap, microorganisms—bacteria and fungi so small they can be seen only with a microscope—are what decompose the biodegradable material. They exude chemicals that dissolve the organic matter, and then absorb or soak up the resulting chemical solution through the surfaces of their bodies. If a compost heap works well and the microorganisms are given enough time to decompose everything, the resulting dark, powdery material is something wonderful called humus. Other than plenty of air, water, and nutrients, humus is the most desirable thing you can have in your gar-

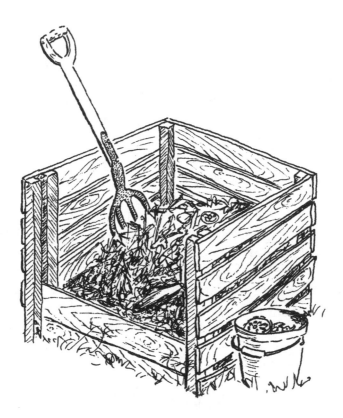

Partially enclosed compost bins like this one need their sides open enough to allow air to freely enter. If composting material aquires a powdery, gray coating, add more water; if it turns black and stinks like a sewer, spade it more frequently and don't keep it as moist.

den soil. The main reason humus is so desirable is that it improves a soil's ability to hold water and nutrients and to be worked.

1. If you want the nutrient-rich water that seeps from the future heap to soak in where the heap is standing, loosen the soil below the future heap by tilling or spading it up.
2. Connect the ends of a ten-foot section of two- or four-inch mesh wire fence about three feet high, forming an upright cylinder.
3. At the bottom of the wire cylinder, arrange a layer of organic material. If the organic material is mostly dense, moist matter, such as

overly mature garden produce and kitchen trimmings, a loose layer of about two inches will do. If it is mostly dry material, such as straw or dry leaves, make a layer three to four inches deep.

4. Add an activator. If employing a concentrated form of nitrogen, such as alfalfa meal, bone meal, or dry, high-protein dog food, sprinkle on a large handful; if using barnyard manure, scatter about a shovelful, with a shovelful of rich dirt atop that; if using store-bought activator, follow directions on the box.

5. Repeat the above two steps until you reach the top of the fence or run out of organic material.

6. Moisten the pile thoroughly, but don't soak it. During the heap's entire life, keep it moist; during hot, dry summers, you may need to hose it down every three or four days.

7. If there's room, add organic material as it becomes available, repeating steps 3 and 4. Be sure to keep the center loose so that air can circulate.

8. In a week, remove the wire. Lift it over the heap if you can, or else detach the wire ends and unwrap it from around the heap. Next to the free-standing heap, re-erect the wire cylinder, and fork all the material back into it. Try to place the outside, drier material inside the new pile. This is the time to appraise how your heap has been doing. If it looks dry and uncooked, you'll need to become more conscientious with your watering. You may need to sprinkle in more activator.

9. In two more weeks, you should have fairly coarse mulch appropriate for spreading around tomatoes or mixing into the soil. If you want a finer, richer material, repeat the above step until the compost is the way you want it.

Observe Effects of Particle Size on Soil

The soil is that part of the garden ecosystem where the subtle and not-so-subtle workings of chemistry are most manifest. Soil scientists often refer to *the soil solution*, because much more than dirt, soil is a solution of living things and chemical compounds interacting in intimate and significant ways.

A soil's character—its workability, its richness, its ability to hold water and many other features—depends very much on the relative amounts of sand, silt, and clay present in it. Soil particle size also very much affects a soil's nutrient-holding capacity. Nutrients are chemical elements, such as nitrogen, phosphorus, potassium, calcium, iron, and magnesium that the plants in our lawns and gardens absolutely must have in order to live. The following project explores soil's water-holding capacity.

1. Fill one pot with dry sand and the other with an equal amount of silt or clay. Dust is fine clay—look for it where the soil is sheltered from rain. You'll know it's dust if it feels soapy, not gritty, between your fingers. If you can't find dry dust, just use any dry dirt you can find composed of very small mineral particles.

2. Slowly pour water into each pot, keeping track of how much water you're using, until it begins to run through the drainage hole; if water pools atop the silt or clay, stir it into the soil.

3. Much, much less water should have been needed in the sand-filled pot than in the silt- or clay-filled pot before it began draining out. From the results of your experiment, do you agree with the statement that the smaller average grain size of a particular soil, the more water it holds? If your garden plants are wilting too soon after watering because of a problem with soil particle size, is the situation caused by soil particles being too large (sandy soil) or too small (clayey soil)?

Observe Effects of Organic Matter on Soil Structure

When organic matter is mixed into garden soil, it eventually is decomposed by soil microorganisms, fungi, and earthworms into a dark, moist material resembling powdered charcoal. This material, called humus, is dispersed throughout the soil. In soil, humus particles behave like clay particles in their ability to hold nutrients and water; they also improve the soil texture and make it more workable. Thus, humus is a gardener's secret weapon.

1. Fill one pot and half fill another with dry clay soil or dust.
2. Add a half pot of dry humus-rich soil, potting soil, peat, or well-digested compost to the half pot of dry clay soil, and thoroughly mix.
3. Pour a cup of water into each pot.
4. Place the pots in a warm or hot dry place with good ventilation, and wait until the soils dry out. (This may take a week or more.)
5. Compare the dried-out contents. The soil composed of nothing but tiny clay particles should dry into a very hard, bricklike substance; the soil into which organic matter has been mixed should be much more granular and workable—it should have a better soil texture.

Test Insect Aversion to Marigolds and Garlic

Often there is no elegant way to protect our tomatoes or any other garden plant from the myriad of insects and other animals that want to eat them before we get a chance. At some point, every gardener must decide where on the pest control spectrum he or she resides. Organic gardeners eschew using synthetic chemicals for health and environmental reasons. Even gardeners filled with reverence for life, however, have certain tricks for dealing with garden pests.

It is often said that marigolds and garlic keep insects off nearby plants. To find out if this is true, conduct your own experiment.

1. Early in the spring, choose a type of plant in your garden that usually is vigorously attacked by insects (snap beans and potatoes are good candidates). Thickly plant marigolds and garlic in and around part of this year's crop. If you have pole-bean tepees, plant marigolds and garlic inside and around some tepees but not others; if you have rows, plant around one end but not the other.

2. At the peak of bug season in late summer, choose five plants far from any marigolds and garlic, and count the number of bugs on them. Make a breakdown of bug species if you can. Then calculate the average number of bugs per plant by dividing the number of bugs by the number of plants.

3. Now do the same thing for five plants in a part of the garden thickly planted with marigolds and garlic. Try to examine garden plants of similar size in each sample, because larger plants would probably harbor more insects, and that would throw off your calculations.

4. Write your results in your backyard nature notebook, and if your experimental technique has been good and your results are dramatic, let people know what you found out. Write to the local newspaper and even contact local radio and television crews, for people like to know about these things.

4

AT SUNDOWN

Focus on Smells

Humans have been called "eye-dependent" because in the lighted world of day, we receive information primarily through sight. We see clouds scuttling across the sky—their shape and color tell us to expect fair weather or a storm. We delight in the variety of birds that visit our backyard feeders, which we identify by their shape, color, and size. We speak of colorful wildflowers that fill the meadows and of the beautifully shaped trees that line the streets. Even at night we tend to focus our attention on what we can and cannot see.

Many night animals depend on smell more than any other sense. We don't often recognize smell for what it is—a chemical sense that, along with taste, gives living things the ability to detect chemicals in their environment. Animals have a chemical-detection sense that picks up molecules released by many objects into the air. You experience this every time you smell the fragrance of your favorite perfume, detect the aroma of food cooking, or pick up odors that may not be so pleasant. Like other mammals, we have special detection cells in our nasal passages.

Scientists from different specialties agree that over the years we human beings have become less dependent on our ability to discriminate odors. Unlike our ancestors, who had to use every sense fully in order to simply stay alive, our talent for identifying and remembering the huge number of odors that bombard our olfactory receptors has diminished. Nocturnal insects and animals, however, continue to sniff their way through the night to find food and mates—and to avoid danger.

1. The night air carries many odors. Sit undisturbed for about fifteen minutes and concentrate on the smells that surround you. What specific odors can you detect? You may not be able to identify all of them. Try to compare these with familiar odors. If you conduct your first census after a long, hot, dry period, do it again when it is hot and humid. What differences did you notice? Is cold weather better or worse than warm for detecting odors?

2. If a breeze is blowing, put your nose close to the ground. Can you pick up more odors than when you are seated? What seems to be the best height for different odors? As you repeat the activity do you notice an improvement in your skill? Once you have sharpened your olfactory skills you can practice anywhere: in the city, in the suburbs, or at the shore.

3. Hold a handful of litter such as leaves, moss, and soil and smell it. Describe the odor. How does it change if the litter is wet, as it would be after a rain? Taste and smell are closely related senses. Can you "taste" the odors?

4. Smells are often responsible for helping us reach back into our personal history. The memories are often pleasant, but the fragrances may also remind us of unhappy times. Keep a record of odors and past events they caused you to remember. Some of us are more successful at this than others. How is your fragrance recall?

Listen to the Night

First let's examine the nature of sound. You have seen the wonderful effects caused by falling dominoes; each one knocks over its neighbor, causing a moving "wave." Sound travels through the air in a similar way. If someone on the other side of the room drops a book onto the floor, the energy caused by this event strikes air molecules, causing them to vibrate and bump their neighbor molecules. The wave of energy passes from one molecule to another until it reaches your ears.

Hearing occurs when this mechanical energy is trapped by our ear flaps (pinnae) and transmitted through our middle ear to our inner ear. Through a complex process the mechanical energy is transformed into electrical energy in the inner ear and sent to the brain. In the section of the brain specialized to process this energy, the vibrations are interpreted as specific sounds.

You have heard the varied voices of living things fill the night as they send messages to others of their own kind. Bats, nighthawks, skunks, insects, frogs, and other creatures respond to various cues in

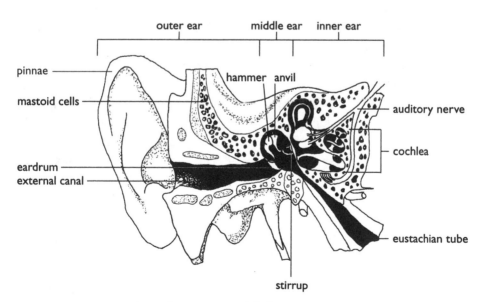

Cutaway view of the human ear

the environment such as temperature, humidity, and level of darkness. The process is well ordered, not random, and is consistent night after night.

1. Sit quietly for thirty minutes or so and listen to the night. You will probably be aware of some familiar sounds such as the bark of a dog, the voices of children, or the wail of a cat. Listen for more unfamiliar sounds such as the rustle of a field mouse foraging in the leaf litter, the songs of crickets, or the hoot of an owl.

   Keep a record of what you hear and the time you hear it. Repeat this exercise for several nights. Is there an order to the sounds you hear, or do the noises occur randomly? Did you find a pattern? Is that splash in the pond part of the pattern, or was it simply an anomaly?

2. It is said that sounds travel farther at night than during the day. Perhaps this is related to humidity or temperature, or perhaps this is just because we listen more carefully when we cannot see very well. Can you design an investigation that would help you to figure out if sound really travels farther at night?

3. Listen to the soft whisper of the wind blowing gently through a pine grove. Compare it with the hissing, pulsating winter wind that whips through the woodland. How would you describe the sound of wind blowing through dry leaves? Listen for other voices of the wind and describe them.

4. Some night sounds are fairly loud like the cricket symphony, but others, like the churring of a foraging skunk, are faint and require us to get close to the source. Some are unexpected, like the snap of a twig or the sudden rustle of leaf litter. Be alert for new sounds as you listen to the night. Listen for sudden silences. What are their causes? Are these just pockets of silence? Can you make some of the calling stop? How long does it take for the sounds to begin again?

5. The ears of nocturnal animals show some interesting adaptations. You may have to visit a zoo or wildlife center that keeps live animals. Watch the animals as they sit, lie down, or eat. Describe their ear flaps. Are they large or small in relation to the size of the animal's head? Are the ear flaps covered or lined with fur, or are they

naked or nearly so? Does the animal move its ear flaps as it rests quietly or as it eats? Do both ear flaps always move in the same direction at the same time? Can the animal direct one of its ear flaps in one direction while the other ear is pointed in another direction? What advantage is this for the animal?

6. Dogs hear very well and can pick up the sound of something approaching long before we do. Spend some time observing a dog. What does it do with its ear flaps as it picks up sounds? Does it move its head or its ear flaps as it tries to figure out where the sound is coming from? Can the dog change the direction of the ear flaps, or must it turn its head? If you cannot find a dog to watch, observe a cat or a squirrel.

Find an Owl Roost

Finding owl roosts can be a challenge for even the most persistent, but knowing where to search and what to look for will increase your chances of a successful hunt. After a night of foraging, owls return to their roosts to sleep. Because owls generally roost in the same trees each night, the trunks are often streaked white with bird lime. Search the bare branches of these marked trees and you may find a sleeping owl or a hollow that the owl calls home.

Other evidence of a roosting owl is a collection of gray, furry two-inch-long bundles at the base of a tree. Called owl pellets, these contain the undigested material from an owl meal and tell you that an owl has been there. If you search dilapidated buildings such as old barns, you will probably find some pellets scattered over the ground or piled beneath beams the owls use to roost.

Analyze Owl Pellets

Owls do not chew their food. If the prey are small, owls will swallow them whole, but if the animals are large (like rabbits), owls will tear them with their sharp beaks into pieces that can be swallowed more easily. Owls' digestive enzymes cannot break down materials such as fur, feathers, bones, and the chitinous material of insect exoskeletons. These waste materials are pressed into neat bundles by the bird's strong stomach muscles. The bird regurgitates the packages and drops them onto the woodland floor. These pellets, which come in various shades of gray and brown, are two to three-and-a-half inches long and one inch in diameter.

1. When you find some pellets, put them in a plastic sandwich bag and label it with the location, date, time of day, and weather conditions.

2. Pellets can collect bacteria and other small organisms, so leave them wrapped in the plastic bag or place them in a sealed container and put them in your freezer for two weeks. When you finish

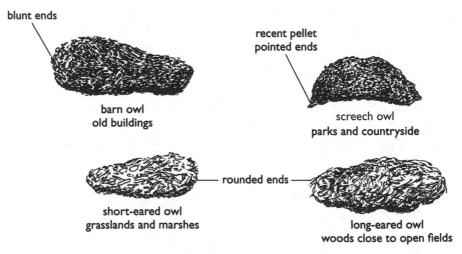

blunt ends

recent pellet
pointed ends

barn owl
old buildings

screech owl
parks and countryside

rounded ends

short-eared owl
grasslands and marshes

long-eared owl
woods close to open fields

The shape of a pellet and the place where it was found help to identify the species of owl that produced it.

working with the pellets, wash your hands. If you are unable to find any pellets, you can buy them from biological supply houses at a very modest cost.

3. What color is your pellet? What are its length and width? Can you see any objects in the pellet, or is it solid fur? Make a drawing of your pellet.

4. You will need a pair of tweezers, a darning needle, and a bowl of water. The pellets are easier to tease apart when wet, and there is less danger of breaking the bones inside. Use a hand lens to find tiny bones you may have overlooked. If you have enough pellets, you might want to try opening a dry pellet. You will be surprised at how tightly packed it is.

5. With a pair of tweezers, remove the bones from the fur ball and put them on a piece of white paper so that you can keep track of them. Keep the bowl of water on hand to swish the bones clean of debris.

6. What colors can you detect in the fur? Gray? Black? Brown? White? Other?

7. Look for similarities and differences among the bones you find in owl pellets. With the help of the chart on the next page, group bones of the same kind together. How many shoulder blades do you find? How many hip bones? Vertebrae? Hind legs or parts of hind legs? Forelegs or parts of forelegs? Ribs? Do you see any similarities between the bones in your pellets and human bones?

8. You can disinfect the bones by swishing them in a bleach solution. Don't leave them in the bleach too long or you might damage them.

9. After you have cleaned and disinfected the bones, make a display of them by gluing them onto a piece of oak tag. This makes it easier to compare them. Look for differences in hip skeletons, skulls, jawbones, and so forth.

10. Can you infer from the number of skulls in a pellet the number of prey the owl ate? Will the number of legs provide you with the same kind of information? Which is the more accurate predictor for the actual number of prey eaten by the owl? How many prey do you find in your pellets? In your pellet sample, what is the greatest number of prey in a pellet? The lowest number? The average number of prey?

BONES IN THE PELLET

Example	Bones	Tally
	skull	
	jaw	
	ribs	
	hip	
	shoulder blade	
	hind legs	
	front legs	
	vertebrae	

(Examples not to scale)

11. Make a bar graph to show the relationship between the number of forelegs, hind legs, and skulls. What information does the graph give you about these relationships?

Observe a Frog's Life Cycle

People tend to lump all frogs into a few simple categories—pond frogs versus toads, big frogs versus little frogs—but the world of nature is much more complicated than that. Scientists have organized frogs into several groups: tailed frogs, narrow-mouthed toads, spadefoot toads, true toads, cricket frogs, chorus frogs, tree frogs, and true frogs.

- Spadefoot toads—eastern spadefoot toad (*Scaphiopus holbrooki*)
- True toads—American toad (*Bufo americanus*)
- Tree frogs—spring peeper (*Pseudacris crucifer*), gray tree frog (*Hyla versicolor*)
- True frogs—eastern wood frog (*Rana sylvatica*), northern leopard frog (*R. pipiens*), green frog (*R. clamitans*), bullfrog (*R. catesbeiana*)

These representative frogs have a wide range east of the Rocky Mountains. You can find other species in your locality by consulting a field guide to amphibians.

You can observe the life cycle of a frog from egg to adult by setting up a simple aquarium and putting some frog eggs in it. Frogs lay their jelly-coated eggs in fresh water. Look for them in a pond, puddle, bog, swamp, or any other wet area where frogs breed. Look for the gelatinous masses often tangled in pond vegetation. The egg masses of some species have such buoyancy that they will float in water.

1. If you can find some eggs, scoop up a few and put them into a wide-mouthed container. Three or four eggs are enough. When they hatch you can transfer the tadpoles to a larger container. Because tadpoles are sensitive to chlorine and the iron that leaches from water pipes, be sure to use pond water rather than tap water for your aquarium.

2. Although you have probably seen tadpoles swimming in ponds, you may not have observed them in an orderly way. A good way to begin systematic observation is to capture one or two tadpoles and

Life cycle of a frog

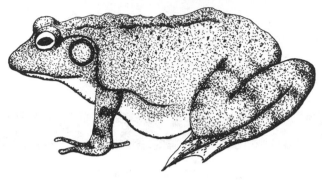

6. The plant-eating tadpole has changed into an insect-eating frog—an adult capable of reproducing.

1. The female lays soft, jelly-covered eggs in the water of a pond, and they are fertilized by the male.

5. Gills are replaced with lungs; the mouth and eyes change and the tail is absorbed.

2. A tiny, fishlike tadpole hatches from an egg.

3. The tadpole breathes through feathery gills that grow on each side of the head. These quickly disappear, to be replaced by internal gills.

4. The hind legs grow first. The front legs grow under the skin and then break through.

observe their structure and their behavior. You can scoop tadpoles out of the pond with a fine mesh net, available in any shop that sells home aquarium supplies. Wear a pair of old sneakers, as you may need to wade into the water.

3. After capturing the tadpoles, put them into a large container that allows them to swim freely. A wide-mouthed gallon jar is sufficient for two or three tadpoles. Add enough water from the pond where you found the tadpoles so that the jar is about three-quarters full.

4. Place the temporary aquarium in a bright area, but avoid direct sunlight. This will give the algae—the tadpoles' food—sufficient light for growth. Don't try to clean the pond water by straining out the tiny particles of dead and decaying plant material, because the tadpoles eat this material as well.

5. Write a description of a tadpole. What is it doing? With the help of a hand lens, you can discover how a newly hatched tadpole hangs on to plants. What is happening to the tail? Look for the feathery external gills on either side of the tadpole. How do you think it breathes? When do the external gills disappear? When do the hind legs appear? Does the tadpole seem to be gulping air at the water's surface? What is a possible explanation for this behavior? Did your tadpole stop eating? What might be happening?

Build a Frog Terrarium

Frogs can be kept in a terrarium for a short period of time without suffering harm, but because toads are less dependent on water, you may want to use them instead. When you are handling a frog be sure your hands are wet, because hot, dry hands can harm the frog's delicate skin.

1. You can use a ten-gallon or larger aquarium for adult frogs. Put a rectangular plastic food-storage container into the aquarium and fill it with pond water. A two-cup size will work well. To supply the frog with fresh water, simply remove the container, clean it, and fill it with water.

2. Into the remaining space put some gravel and cover it with potting soil. Add woodland litter such as a few rocks, some moss, pieces of

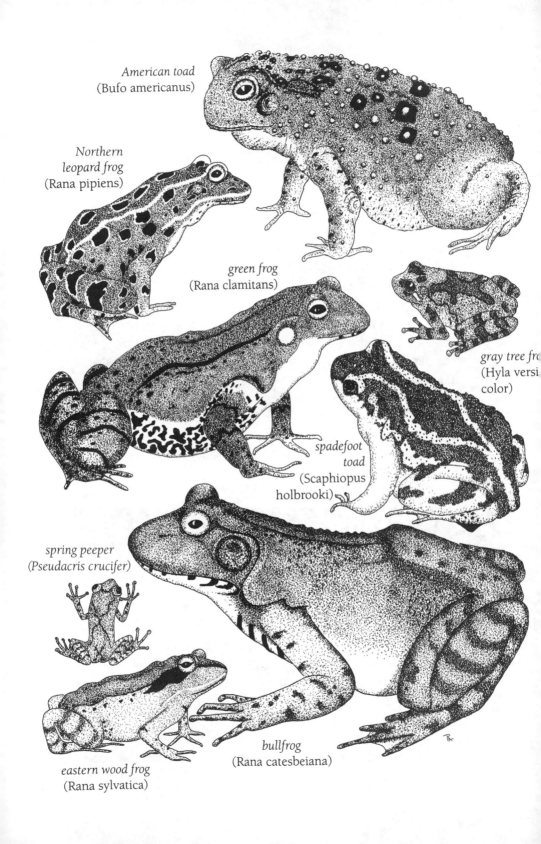

American toad
(Bufo americanus)

Northern
leopard frog
(Rana pipiens)

green frog
(Rana clamitans)

gray tree fr[
(Hyla versi
color)

spadefoot
toad
(Scaphiopus
holbrooki)

spring peeper
(Pseudacris crucifer)

bullfrog
(Rana catesbeiana)

eastern wood frog
(Rana sylvatica)

bark, small branches, and twigs. Finish your temporary frog habitat by placing a piece of screening over the top of the tank to prevent the frog from leaping out.

3. To feed your frog, you must supply it with live, active insects. A frog will not eat anything that does not move, no matter how hungry it may be. If you give it flying, wiggling insects such as crickets, flies, moths, caterpillars, slugs, snails, and worms, the frog will eat.

4. Make some additional observations about its structure and its behavior. For example, does the frog keep its eyes open when it eats? How does it sit? Write a description of a sitting frog. How many vocal sacs does it have? Where are they located?

5. When you finish your observations, be sure to return the frog to where you found it.

Swing a Light across a Moth's Path

There are more than ten thousand moth species in North America. You will discover that moths come in a variety of sizes, shapes, colors, and patterns. You will also find out that every generalization made about moths and their families is accompanied by many exceptions.

Most moths are active from dusk to dawn. To gather moths, hang a white sheet over the outside of a lighted window and turn off all other lights in the vicinity. Moths and other insects of the night will cling to your sheet.

You can also hunt for moths in a garden using a flashlight whose beam is covered with red or yellow cellophane. As you shine the flashlight around the flowers you may spot the copper glint of moth eyes (from the Noctuidae family of moths) as the creatures feed on flowers.

Most people know that moths are attracted to a stationary light, but do moths respond in a similar way if the light is swinging?

1. Find a place where you can sit comfortably for about twenty minutes.

2. Swing a lighted flashlight back and forth with the beam of light pointing skyward. How do the moths behave? Explain their behavior.

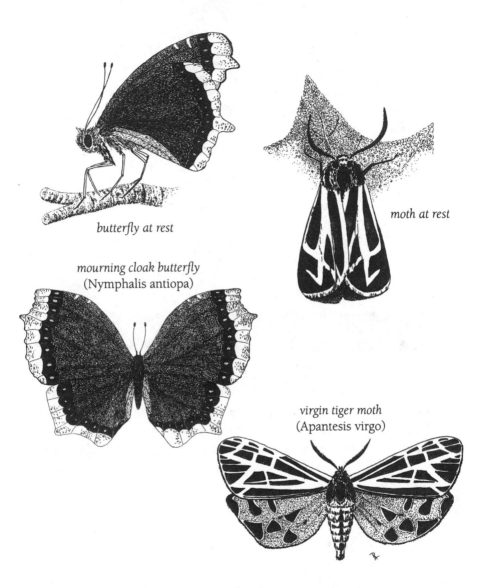

butterfly at rest

moth at rest

mourning cloak butterfly
(Nymphalis antiopa)

virgin tiger moth
(Apantesis virgo)

Butterflies and moths have so many similar characteristics that it's sometimes difficult to tell them apart.

Attract Moths with Sugaring

Not all moths are attracted to light, but you can entice light-shy moths to your neighborhood with a technique called sugaring. For this activity you will need to prepare a sweet and somewhat smelly brew.

1. Mix a can of beer with one pound of dark sugar. Add one or two very ripe bananas, one-half cup molasses, one-half cup fruit juice, and one shot of rum. Mix thoroughly.

2. Pour into a large container and let it mellow outdoors for a few days. To keep the flies out of your concoction, lay a cloth over the top of the jar.

3. Next, saturate some dishwashing sponges with the potion and hang them from tree branches, fence posts, or posts you erect in your garden. (Moths will not come if your sponges are in open fields.) You could also smear the concoction on tree trunks with a paint-brush.

4. The best time to start "sugaring" is on a warm, still, starless night. Check your sponges frequently. If you want to examine the moths you attract, trap them in a container with a lid and place the container in the refrigerator (not the freezer) for several hours or overnight. This will make the moth very sluggish. When you remove the chilled moth, you can observe it at your leisure. Of course, as the moth warms up, it will begin to move and will soon become as active as it was when you caught it.

Study Fireflies

Fireflies are beetles, members of the insect order Coleoptera. The name of the order comes from the Greek word for "sheath" (*koleon*), which reflects the leathery quality of their outer wings. Like many other insects, beetles have two pairs of wings—forewings and hind wings—but beetles don't use their forewings (called elytra) for flying. In flight the beetles spread the elytra and use them for balance. When they are not flying, beetles use the elytra to cover and protect the delicate membranous flight wings.

Fireflies are excellent subjects for you to observe because you can do so without interfering with their lives. Participation in the following activities will not make you an expert, but you will discover that the world of this little beetle is very complex. You might even decide that you would like to go beyond this section and learn more about them.

1. Local weather conditions such as the amount of precipitation during the winter and early spring often determine when fireflies begin to emerge each spring from where they overwintered as larvae and pupae. Record the date of your first sighting and keep a record of the fireflies' arrival over a period of a few years.

2. With a sweep net or a swift and gentle hand, scoop up a few fireflies and put them in a clear container with a lid (a mayonnaise jar will do nicely). Punch some holes from the inside of the lid outward so that the fireflies don't scrape against the rough edges of the holes.

3. Find the two big insect eyes that are typical of many kinds of night fliers. How long are the antennae? Are they smooth or saw toothed? How many legs are there? Are they long or short? What does the length of the legs tell you about the firefly's lifestyle? Look at the underside of the beetle. Describe the abdomen. Is it ivory or glazed looking or perhaps yellowish? On what segments are the lamps? Make a drawing of your firefly and keep it in your notebook.

4. The patterns of firefly flashes differ in a number of ways. With the help of a stopwatch and a friend, follow a firefly for several minutes. What can you find out about its flashes? How long is it between sig-

nals? On average, how far does the firefly travel between each signal? How long do signals last? Does the light produce a pattern?

5. Do you live in an area where there are yellow-flashing and green-
flashing fireflies? You may notice that these two kinds of fireflies are
active in different degrees of darkness. The fireflies that flash yellow
lights are generally active during the early evening hours. At this
time their yellow lights will contrast with the green foliage of the
surrounding trees and shrubs, making it easier for the fireflies to
see one another. Fireflies with green lamps wait until it becomes
darker before beginning to flash their mating codes.

6. Most fireflies in the northern temperate zone wink their lights
unless they are in stressful situations. Capture one and hold it in
your hand. Does it blink its light, or is there a steady glow from the
firefly lamp?

7. Capture a moth, a cricket, and a firefly. Put each into a separate see-
through container (a bug box is a good choice). Compare the wings
of your captives. Do they have scales? Are they opaque or transparent? How many pairs of wings does each insect have? How do these

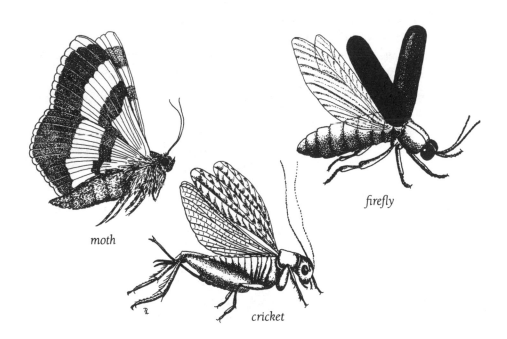

firefly

moth

cricket

sets of wings differ? Where are the wings located? Look for the veins in the wings. The patterns formed by the veins are important characteristics that scientists use when they are trying to identify closely related species of insects. Make a drawing of each insect and its wings.

8. A male firefly signals from on high, using his large eyes to scan the night, which is alive with winking and blinking lights. Can you find a male and female pair signaling each other? Look for a signal from a male that seems to be honing in on a ground signal. Follow that male and see if you can find the responding female. Females are extremely difficult to locate, but you can sometimes find one by crawling around on a recently cut lawn.

Build a Bat House

Except for the nectar-drinking, pollen-eating long-nosed bats (*Leptonycteris* spp.) of the southwestern United States, which forage during the day, most North American bats wait until twilight to begin hunting for insects. Although large roosts are easier to find than small ones, locating any daytime hangouts can be very difficult. Bats that roost in churches, houses, barns, and other buildings generally give away their presence with a brown stain caused by their droppings running down the side of the building. Another sign of bats is the whitish guano that collects on the ground below a roost. Another good way to locate bats is to ask a naturalist at a nature center about local bat populations. Some of the North American bats that prefer group living and congregate in buildings are the evening bat (*Nycticeius humeralis*), the big brown bat (*Eptesicus fuscus*), the little brown bat (*Myotis lucifugus*), and the pallid bat (*Antrozous pallidus*).

Some bats shun both buildings and caves and seek the solitude offered by a hollow tree, or simply hang from tree branches. Asleep in the cool shadows of the foliage, these bats usually go unnoticed because they resemble dead leaves. The eastern pipistrelle (*Pipistrellus subflavus*), the most abundant bat in the eastern United States, prefers

silver-haired bat
(Lasionycteris noctivagans)

red bat
(Lasiurus borealis)

eastern pipistrelle
(Pipistrellus subflavus)

hoary bat
(Lasiurus cinereus)

to roost in sycamore trees, but they're extremely difficult to find. The red bat, the silver-haired bat, and the hoary bat also like to hide in trees and shrubs.

Many bats are losing their natural roosts. Building a bat house is one way you can encourage these friendly creatures of the night to come into your backyard.

The directions for the bat house are taken from *America's Neighborhood Bats* by Merlin D. Tuttle. Do not use chemically treated wood for any part of your bat house.

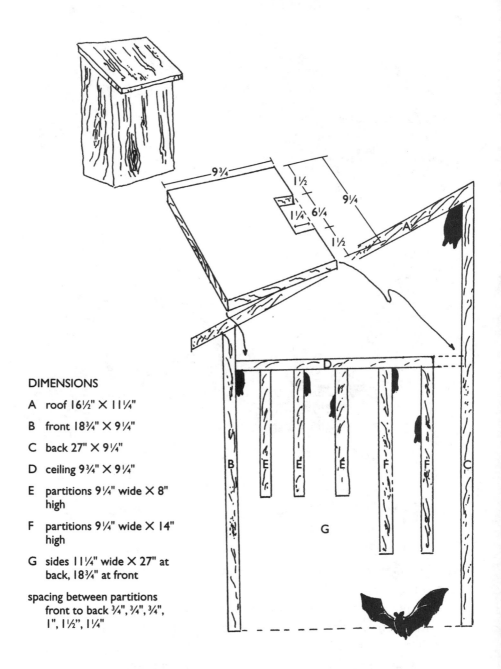

DIMENSIONS

A roof 16½" × 11¼"

B front 18¾" × 9¼"

C back 27" × 9¼"

D ceiling 9¾" × 9¼"

E partitions 9¼" wide × 8"
   high

F partitions 9¼" wide × 14"
   high

G sides 11¼" wide × 27" at
   back, 18¾" at front

spacing between partitions
   front to back ¾", ¾", ¾",
   1", 1½", 1¼"

Use rough lumber and turn the rough sides of the roof, front, back, and sides inward. Cut ⅟₁₆ inch horizontal grooves at ½-inch intervals on smooth sides of partitions.

Examine Grasshoppers

Grasshoppers are found wherever there are grasses—in the desert, at the seashore, and in the mountains. They are most abundant in warm and sunny areas such as fields, meadows, and prairies. Crickets and katydids frequent these habitats as well, but these hoppers achieve their greatest diversity in woodlands. Throughout the ages these insects have been part of man's surroundings and, sometimes, their diets. Although they are no longer desirable in Western cuisine, this may change. At a "bug banquet" hosted by the New York Entomological Society, guests dined on cricket and vegetable tempura. Grasshopper soup was featured at the annual meeting of another science society.

Our relationship with grasshoppers has not always been so satisfying. A brief review of history tells us that grasshoppers can be a scourge. Great swarms of them periodically devour every green thing in farmlands of Asia and Africa and on the American plains. They have fed from these and other banquet tables since long before the biblical plagues of locusts (grasshoppers) in Egypt.

Because grasshoppers are most abundant in late summer and autumn, plan to observe them at this time. A good way to begin systematic observation is to capture a grasshopper.

1. Take a walk in a grassy field or meadow and scores of insects will fly up from the grass as you move through it. Catch a grasshopper with an insect net or your hand. When you have a captive or two, put each directly into a plastic sandwich bag so that you can observe and compare them.

2. Grasshoppers are large (especially if you trap them late in the season), usually easy to capture, and survive well in a container for a short period of time. Take a close look at your grasshopper, and with the help of the illustration discover some of the physical features that make this insect work so well in its environment.

3. With the help of a hand lens, look for the jaws (mandibles and maxillae). Watch as the hopper eats a blade of grass.

4. Grasshoppers have two sets of eyes. This is handy because the grasshopper cannot adjust its eyes for far and near vision in the way that we can. The two large compound eyes are for distance

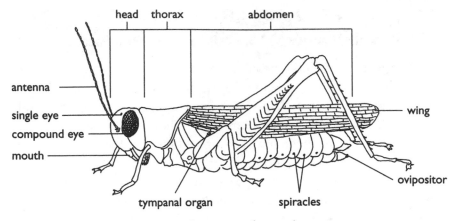

External structure of a grasshopper

vision and are composed of thousands of little lenses and other eye parts. Compare the eyes in the illustration with those of the grasshopper you have caught.

5. Are the antennae longer or shorter than the grasshopper's body? If they are longer, how much longer are they? With the help of a hand lens, you can see the many joints that make the antennae so flexible. What does the insect do with the antennae? Put some food in the path of the grasshopper so that the antennae can reach it. What happens?

6. A grasshopper has six legs. The first pair is short. Watch as the grasshopper walks up the side of a glass. Look for hairy pads on each claw. The hairs secrete a sticky liquid that prevents the hopper from slipping when walking on smooth surfaces. The second pair of legs is somewhat longer than the first. The third pair is long and muscular and ideal for jumping. Look for double pairs of spines on the back of each hind foot. These aid in jumping by digging into the ground like the cleats on a sprinter's shoes.

7. A usual pattern when walking is for the grasshopper to take two steps forward, then stop; take another two steps forward, then stop; and so forth. If the hind legs are moving slowly, the other legs are moving at a similar pace. What happens to the front legs when the hind legs are moving more rapidly?

8. The abdomen is divided into segments. Do the rings go around the entire body? Lift the wings and find the hearing organ on the first segment of the abdomen.

   Look for breathing pores along the side of the abdomen. How many are there?

9. Look carefully and you will see the abdomen move rhythmically up and down. If one up-and-down cycle equals one breath, how many breaths does a grasshopper take each minute? Is this the same number of breaths that you take each minute, or is it more or fewer?

10. While you are observing your grasshoppers, you may be able to watch the grooming process. Does there appear to be a sequence to the process, or is it haphazard? How does the grasshopper clean its antennae, its wings, its legs, and its body?

11. If you want to continue your observations at home, transfer your grasshoppers to a larger container such as a wide-mouthed gallon jar. Put a small handful of grasses into the jar to supply the grasshoppers with food and a familiar habitat. Fill a small vial with water and use a piece of cotton as a stopper, making sure the end of the cotton is in contact with the water. Capillary action will draw the water into the cotton so that the grasshoppers can drink from it.

5

IN WINTER

Snow crystals are born in high-altitude clouds tens of thousands of feet above the earth's surface, where the temperature is between 32 and minus 40°F. The clouds are made up of water vapor in the form of fog or mist. They are composed of microscopic water molecules suspended in air. These water droplets are so small that millions of them could fit on the head of a pin. Clouds are visible because so many million trillion (quintillion) water droplets are concentrated in one area. When you walk through a fog or mist, you have had firsthand experience with a cloud.

1. Before you plan to catch snowflakes, put a piece of dark construction paper or fabric in the freezer.
2. When it snows, place the frozen paper or fabric on a piece of sturdy cardboard for support, and allow the snowflakes to fall on the dark surface.
3. Examine the snowflakes with a hand lens. Some snowflakes may look like fluffy pieces of lint; others may be ice crystals. Draw or describe the snowflakes you "caught" in your notebook.

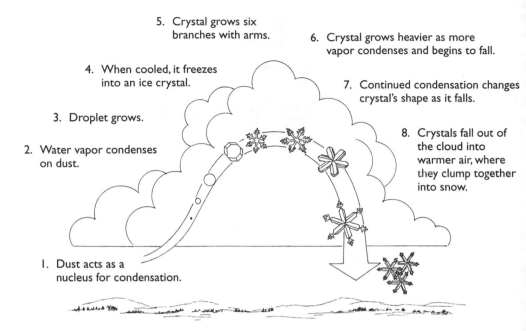

5. Crystal grows six branches with arms.

6. Crystal grows heavier as more vapor condenses and begins to fall.

4. When cooled, it freezes into an ice crystal.

7. Continued condensation changes crystal's shape as it falls.

3. Droplet grows.

8. Crystals fall out of the cloud into warmer air, where they clump together into snow.

2. Water vapor condenses on dust.

1. Dust acts as a nucleus for condensation.

How a snowflake is born

4. For a closer look, you will need a microscope, slides, and a clear lacquer spray. Keep the slides and lacquer spray can in a freezer until you are ready to collect the snowflakes.

5. When the snow begins to fall, remove the slides and lacquer from the freezer and put them on a piece of dry cardboard that you have kept outside. This will prevent the heat from your hands from warming the slides and causing the flakes to melt.

6. Spray the slides with lacquer and carry them, on the cardboard, into the falling snow.

7. After you have collected several snowflakes on the slides, put them in a place away from the falling snow but still outside. Let them remain there for an hour or two until the lacquer has dried.

8. With the help of a microscope (40X should work well), you can examine the imprints left by the snowflakes. Draw or describe them in your notebook.

Make a Snow Gauge

Weather reports often tell us how much accumulation we can expect from the next snowfall. You can make a snow gauge to find out how much snow falls in your neighborhood.

1. Tape a ruler to the inside of an empty coffee can. At the start of the next snowstorm put the container outside in an open area away from trees and buildings.

2. When the storm ends, check the ruler to find out how much new snow there is. Is it the same amount the weather reports predicted, or is it more or less? Repeat this investigation for each snowstorm. How much snow falls each time? What is the total accumulation for a week? A month? The winter season? How does the total winter snow accumulation compare with that of last winter? Two years ago? Five years ago? The librarian at your local library can help you locate this information.

3. Record your findings in your field notebook. Make a graph of your discoveries. If you continue your observations of annual snowfall, you may be able to see some patterns. For example, which winter month generally has the greatest amount of snowfall? Which has the least? Keep records for several years. Does the greatest amount of snow fall during the same month each year?

Determine the Purity of Snow

Although you know that snow is made of water, have you ever wondered what else those elegant snowflakes carry as they slowly tumble earthward? To find out, perform this simple test.

1. Place a clean coffee can or wide-mouthed jar in an open space during a snowstorm.

2. When the storm has ended, bring the container indoors where the snow will melt.

3. Put a piece of filter paper, such as a coffee filter, into a kitchen funnel.

4. Slowly pour half of the melted water from the snow through the filter. What remains in the filter after the water has seeped through it? Examine the particles with a hand lens.
5. With a microscope, slides, and cover slips, you can examine the meltwater more closely. Compare the remaining half of the meltwater with the filtered water. Write your observations in your notebook.

Examine Snow's Insulating Properties

Snow is a good insulator and can protect plants and animals from deadly cold. Snow doesn't create heat—it holds what heat is released from the ground. The temperature under the snow at ground level may be a "cozy" 33°F while the air temperature dips below zero. You can

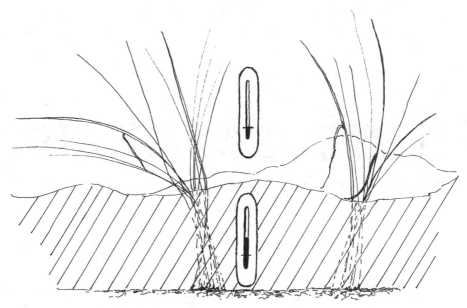

Pushing a thermometer into a snowdrift proves the insulating capacity of snow.

perform a simple test to find out how much protection is provided by about twelve inches of snow.

1. Use an outdoor thermometer to measure the temperature of the air above the snow, then the temperature of the ground.
2. Repeat this for several days. What did you find out? Would deeper snow offer greater insulation? Does the quality of the snow affect the insulating properties? Record your results on a chart.

Turn Snow into Water

Snow is just another form of water that falls from the sky as precipitation. Because snow is simply small ice crystals, the density is less than that of pure water. Examine how snow relates to its liquid form in the following activity.

1. After a snowfall, fill a measuring cup with fresh snow and let it melt, then pour the meltwater into a measuring cup. Keep track of how many cups of snow it takes to make one cup of water.
2. Repeat the investigation for old snow from the middle and bottom of a snowdrift. Does the amount of snow required to make a cup of water depend on the age of the snow? Do you need more or less snow if it is newly fallen? Old snow from the middle of a snowdrift? From the bottom of the snowdrift?
3. Record your results in a notebook.

Observe Color and Snowmelt

Dark objects absorb more heat than light ones. During the day, trees absorb heat from the sun. The trees radiate heat and melt the snow. What are the advantages of this to birds and animals living in that habitat? What other objects in your environment create similar bare spaces around them? For this experiment, you will need same-size squares of construction paper in a variety of colors.

1. Find an area where the snow cover is evenly distributed over flat ground. On a bright, sunny day, place all of the pieces on the snow, weigh each one down with a small stone, and leave them there for at least three hours.

2. Predict which square will sink the deepest into the snow. Which do you think will sink the least? Rank the colors in order of their "melt capacity." How accurate were your predictions?

3. Now repeat the procedure using different pieces of materials such as aluminum foil, unpainted wood, wool, cotton, ceramic tile, linoleum, carpet, and Styrofoam. Be sure all the pieces are the same size. Which material sinks the deepest? Measure to find out.

Record Temperature and Snowmelt

Does the temperature of snow change as it melts? You can find out by recording the temperature of the snow during the melting process.

1. Pack a four-ounce paper cup with snow.

2. Invert the cup on a table and gently squeeze out the snow so that you get an upside-down cup-shaped heap of snow.

3. Record the temperature of the snow every two or three minutes. Make a graph to show your results.

Examine Birch Trees

Birch is a genus of trees and shrubs that represents about fifty species. They are widely scattered throughout the temperate regions of the Northern Hemisphere, where they can grow to a height of thirty to eighty feet. As you begin to explore their world, you will find birches thriving in a variety of habitats, from sun-drenched fields to the moist lowlands of slow-moving rivers. Birch trees also are favorite plantings of homeowners and landscape gardeners, so you probably can find one in your neighborhood.

These trees delight the beginning tree sleuth, because the white bark that distinguishes two of the most widespread species makes them easy to identify as birch trees. There is no mistaking the white, or paper, birch and the gray birch.

Paper birch bark

You can always tell the paper birch (*Betula papyrifera*) by its white, tissue-thin bark that scrolls back from the trunk to reveal bright orange inner bark. This tree has several other common names, which can make things a little confusing. One nickname, canoe birch, reflects a famous use for the bark. The labels white birch and silver birch also are used to describe this tree.

The gray birch (*B. populifolia*) has dull gray-white bark that, in contrast with that of the white birch, hardly peels at all. You can also identify the tree by the black "eyebrows" that develop below the base of branches. Finally, the gray birch is the small birch that grows in fields, and it frequently develops in clusters of several stems that grow from one root system.

Gray birch bark

Yellow birch bark

The bark of the yellow birch (*B. alleghaniensis*) peels in small horizontal scrolls, which, on older trees, makes them look messy. As the tree ages, the color of the bark changes from a bright silvery gray to a reddish or yellowish brown. Look for this tree among sugar maple, American beech, hemlock, red spruce, balsam fir, and white pine. Its preferred habitat is cool with moist soil.

Sweet birch (*B. lenta*) is always scattered among white pine, yellow birch, sugar maple, beech, cherry, white oak, basswood, yellow poplar, and hemlock. Its smooth, dark red to nearly black bark is marked with thin horizontal scars left by old branches. You also can see breathing pores or lenticels on the bark. Break one of the light reddish brown twigs and you will notice the distinct odor of wintergreen.

The range of the river birch (*B. nigra*) extends farther south than that of the other birch trees. Its light reddish bark becomes a flaky silvery gray in older trees and is a clue to their identity. It is the only birch that you will find with nonwhite bark by the riverside.

1. Photographing the bark of each species at different stages in its development will give you a "diary" of the trees as they age. It may

be difficult for you to find a young, middle-aged, and old tree of each birch type in your neighborhood; you may have to go on a treasure hunt as you travel with your parents or friends. Getting a complete set of pictures for each kind of birch tree can take a long time and a lot of observing on your part, but scientists must work.

2. Compared with other trees, birch trees grow fast and have short lives. For example, the life span of the gray birch is only fifty years, and a long-lived birch is about one hundred years old when it dies, compared with the eastern white oak, for example, which lives for about three hundred years. The interiors of dead branches begin to decay very quickly, even while they are still on the tree. Soon a battalion of decay organisms has reduced the interior to mush. If you find some of this dead wood, examine it. What is the decaying material like? What color is it? Is it dry or wet? What is its texture? Can you see any insects in the mushy interior?

Identify Trees by Their Bark

Most people identify trees by their leaves. This makes tree identification a special challenge in winter. This may not be a disadvantage, because it forces you to observe the more subtle differences among trees.

It is difficult to determine the identity of many trees by examining only the bark. One reason for this is that as a tree ages, its bark changes. Nevertheless, there are some trees that have very distinctive bark and are easily recognizable throughout their lives.

1. The sycamore (*Platanus occidentalis*) is easily identified by its mottled and flaking bark. It is frequently planted as a shade tree, and you can find it in parks and along urban and suburban streets.

2. A clue to the nature of the bark of shagbark hickory (*Carya ovata*) lies in the tree's name. Strips of bark scroll away from the trunk and give the tree a shaggy appearance.

3. The bark of the American beech (*Fagus grandifolia*) is smooth and gray or blue-gray.

4. The bark of the American hornbeam (*Carpinus caroliniana*) is often described as resembling flexed arm muscles.

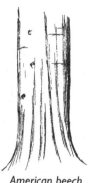

| *American beech* | *Shagbark hickory* | *American hornbeam* | *Sycamore* |
| (Fagus grandifolia) | (Carya ovata) | (Carpinus caroliniana) | (Platanus occidentalis) |

Get Clues from Twigs

Twigs come in a variety of colors, shapes, and sizes. Make a collection starting with beech, oak, shagbark hickory, and maple, if you can find them. How many colors are there among your twigs? Are they straight, zigzag, or curved? Study the additional twig traits described below. The illustrations will help you match twig with tree.

1. First look at the buds. The bud at the tip of the twig is called the terminal bud. As it develops, it adds length to the twig. The buds that grow along the side of the twig are called lateral buds. They produce flowers, leaves, or new branches. Each bud is covered by overlapping scales that protect the developing tissue.

2. The characteristics of the terminal bud can help you identify the tree. Is the bud single or in a cluster? Is it large or small? Pointed or rounded? Hairy? Sticky? What color is it? Oak twigs have clusters of three or four terminal buds protected by brown or reddish brown scales. Beech tree twigs have only one terminal bud. Like the lateral buds, it is shiny tan and cigar shaped. Red maple twigs have a single round, dark red terminal bud. The terminal bud of shagbark hickory is elongated with blunt tips, and is hairy and usually dark brown.

3. Now look at the lateral buds along the sides of the twigs. How do they resemble the terminal buds?

4. The small dots you see on new or young twigs are lenticels. These are openings in the outer layers of the stem and root tissues that

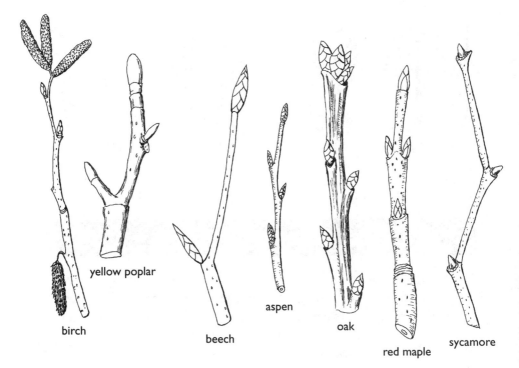

Twigs and buds are especially useful in identifying trees in winter.

allow the exchange of oxygen into and carbon dioxide out of the plant. Is there a pattern to the arrangement of lenticels? How far back on the twig can you find them?

5. Twigs will also show leaf scars. During the summer, the tree produces a layer of cork between the leaf stem and the point where it attaches to the twig. When this layer is complete, the leaf falls, and the mark left on the twig is called the leaf scar. The shape of the leaf scar is unique for each type of tree. You will notice that leaf scars come in a variety of shapes and sizes. The color of the buds also will vary according to the type of tree.

6. The terminal bud scar is the point where the bud scales of the terminal bud were attached. The space between rings, which look like rubber bands around the twig, marks each year's growth. In what year did your twig grow the most? Look at other twigs the same age on the same tree. Do they also show the most growth during that same year?

7. If you cut into a twig, you will find a spongelike substance called pith. When placed in a growth medium, pieces of pith grow into new plants. Cut a cross section of twig and examine the pith. If it is star-shaped, it is probably an oak, poplar, or hickory twig. If the pith is circular, it is probably an elm twig.

Identify Seed Containers

Many deciduous trees retain some seed containers throughout the winter.

1. You can easily see the button balls, or seed clusters, of the sycamore dangling from the zigzag twigs.
2. If you live in an area where sweet gum (*Liquidambar styraciflua*) thrive, look for the spiked seed balls.
3. Ash trees (*Fraxinus* spp.) retain clusters of winged seeds.

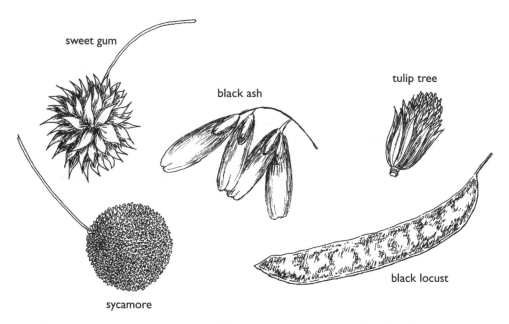

Seed containers come in a variety of shapes and can be used to identify different trees.

4. The yellow poplar or tulip tree (*Liriodendron tulipifera*) produces seed clusters that resemble a tulip blossom. See if you can find these and other trees that retain some seed containers throughout the winter.

Explore Animal Life in Cedars

Today one of the most widespread conifers, or cone-bearing trees, east of the Mississippi is the eastern red cedar. This tree is not as familiar to most people as the members of the pine (Pinaceae) family used to decorate our homes for Christmas. The yellow-green spires of eastern red cedars are also part of the winter landscape, but they get only superficial attention. They are generally looked upon as prickly weed trees that grow in waste places, and it frequently comes as a surprise that they, like pines and spruce, are also cone-bearing trees.

Although we refer to the trees as cedars, botanists tell us that there are no true cedars (*Cedrus* spp.) growing wild in the United States. Cedars grow naturally in North African countries, the Himalayas, and Southeast Asia. Our field tree is actually a juniper and is properly called *Juniperus virginiana*. It is a member of the cedar or cypress family (Cupressaceae) and a close cousin to the arborvitaes and cypresses.

1. Look for throngs of birds such as chickadees, titmice, blue jays, cardinals, juncos, grosbeaks, and sparrows, and for mammals such as raccoons and red and gray squirrels. Do the trees shelter more birds and animals at a particular time of the day?
2. Keep a record for a week or two. Do the birds gather in the trees at any particular time? If birds are in eastern red cedars, are they eating the berries? Which birds do this?
3. Look for red squirrels feeding on pinecones.

Test Tree Sheltering

Do individual trees provide shelter from cold and wind? To find out, you will need two outdoor thermometers, a stick about four feet long, and some string.

1. Put one end of the stick in the ground, and secure one thermometer near the top of the stick.
2. Secure a second thermometer to the main trunk of a cedar tree at the same height above the ground as the thermometer on the stick. What do the two thermometers read?
3. Check them at regular intervals and continue to do so as long into the night as you can. What happens?
4. Put your information on a graph. How do the temperatures compare? Explain your findings.
5. Try this investigation with several other kinds of conifers such as spruce, hemlock, and pine. How do these trees rank against the eastern red cedars as wind protectors?

Examine Seeds and Fruits

The ragged stems you see in your winter travels are the silent remnants of the boisterous weeds and wildflowers whose colors enlivened meadows and roadsides throughout the warmer months. Many of the withered stalks display the intricate framework that supported flower parts; others are simply unadorned sticks.

These stalks and sticks are called winter weeds. They are the remains of plant parts that lived above the ground during the growing season. Although they appear dead, for many of them life goes on below the ground, where strong roots continue to live even in the coldest places. In others, life continues in the form of seeds that wait for the warm rains of spring.

As you explore the world of winter weeds, you will find plants bearing pods. Pods are specialized seed-bearing fruits. Some of the pods will be in reasonably good condition, but others will be torn and ragged from beatings by wind and weather. Achenes, one-seeded fruits, are often difficult for the beginner to distinguish from seeds because they frequently resemble seeds.

With the help of a hand lens, look closely at the silk threads of milkweed and thistle. How are the threads different? Are they separate? Branched? Do you think the difference will affect resistance to wind? You can check your prediction through a simple investigation.

1. Get some milkweed seeds and thistle achenes. With the help of a friend, drop one of each from a height of six feet. How long does it take for each to reach the ground? Repeat this several times and record the data on a chart. *Hint:* Be sure to conduct this experiment in a place free of the slightest breeze.

2. Open the dry flower head of burdock. Are the seeds dispersed by animals or wind? How many achenes (seeds) are there within the bur (fruit)? How do they get out?

3. You can find out approximately how many seeds a winter weed produces by counting them. A milkweed pod would be a good place to begin. Open the pod along the seam, and you will find the seeds arranged like shingles on a roof. Count them. Count the seeds in a few other pods from different milkweed plants, if you can find them. What is the average number of seeds produced by your sample of pods? How many milkweed plants are there in the area? How many milkweed seeds are produced in that place?

4. Find a Queen Anne's lace flower head. The fruits of this common winter weed are found in every tiny umbel that makes up the large umbel blossom, which most people identify as the flower. One person tallied thirty-four umbels, which contained a total of 782 spiny fruits. How many tiny umbels and fruits do you count?

Make a Seed Collection

The chart below will help organize your collection of seeds and fruits.

1. Collect seeds and fruits from many different winter weeds and make a display of them.
2. Record the location of the weeds that produced the seeds and fruits. This is especially helpful if you want to return to find out the identity of the weed.

Weed	Type of Fruit or Seed	Description
Queen Anne's Lace		
Milkweed	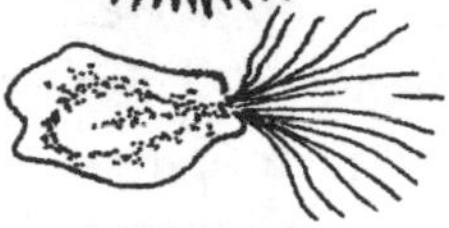	
Dock		
Burdock		
Beggar-ticks		
Joe-pye weed	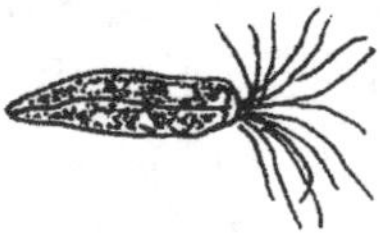	
Mullein		
Pepper grass	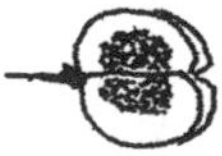	
Tansy		

3. Describe each seed or fruit. A hand lens will help you see detail. Your display will illustrate the range of variation in seed size, design, and adaptation for dispersal.

4. There is a direct relationship between the size of a seed and the amount of food stored in it. Species with large seeds generally produce relatively fewer seeds than those that produce small seeds. What plant produced the smallest seed? The largest seed? Was one shape more common than others?

5. Put the seeds from each different weed in a separate plastic sandwich bag. Label the bags so that you will know which weeds the seeds are from. Later you can attach the seeds to the appropriate place on your display.

6. Draw or photograph each weed to show the unique characteristics of each seed and fruit in your collection. As you examine the seed, you will become aware of the technique each one has for its dispersal. Do they have hooks that will catch on animal fur, tufts of threads, or paper-thin winged membranes that will catch the wind?

7. Add to the list any other winter weeds you find as you explore the world of seeds and fruits. It is said that weeds that produce the most seeds also produce the smallest ones. What do you think?

Construct a Seed Collector

Build a seed collector similar to the one in the diagram.

1. Smear nondrying, sticky Tanglefoot on the plastic covering on the seed collector. Tanglefoot can be found at hardware, garden supply, or farm feed stores. *Caution:* Tanglefoot is very difficult to remove from skin and clothing. Silicone grease on glass plates will trap airborne pollen and also should work for most herbaceous seeds. This arrangement may be easier to use than Tanglefoot.

2. Set the pole of your seed collector in the snow or soil so that the collecting surface is about a foot above the surface of the ground.

3. Orient the direction markers on the collector with the earth's magnetic field. You may need to use a compass.

4. After several days, retrieve your collector. Before you do so, predict which seeds you are most likely to find on its surface. How do your

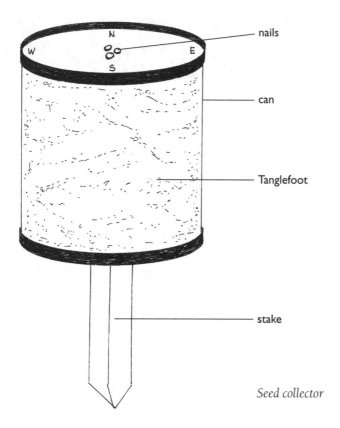

nails

can

Tanglefoot

stake

Seed collector

predictions line up with what you collected? From what compass direction did the most seeds arrive?

5. With the help of your field notes, count and record the number of seeds from each type of weed. You may want to use a hand lens to get a good view of your seeds and to omit any debris such as leaf litter that might have been transported by the wind to your collector.

6. Which were the most common and the least common weed seeds? Which weed species is the most likely to provide food for the birds? Small mammals? You can get a general idea based on the size of the seeds and the quantity of those seeds on your collector. Are there weeds, such as thistle, that supply downy nesting material? What was the direction of the prevailing wind during the time of your collection?

7. Have a friend erect a seed collector a few miles away from yours. Compare your findings. What similarities and differences did you find? What might account for the differences in your findings?

Record Air Temperature and Insect Activity

During the warming days toward the end of winter, the snow around tree trunks seems to come alive. Pepperlike specks on the snow appear and then disappear. The movement occurs so swiftly that it makes the surface of the snow seem fluid. If you put your hand into this snow, the tiny "pepper grains" will leap on and off without leaving a clue as to where they went.

You have witnessed the surface activity of insects called springtails. They are nicknamed snow fleas. Signaled by the right combination of temperature and humidity, these minute insects move up from the soil in huge numbers to the snow's surface around tree trunks and rocks where the snow is partially melted away. They have spent the coldest days of winter beneath the soil litter, feeding on decaying plant material, bits of fungi, and bacteria.

Catching a springtail takes very little skill but a great deal of determination and patience. One way to trap some of these tiny insects is to roll them into a snowball and put it into a sandwich bag. When it is convenient, put some of the bug-packed snow into a bug box and examine it carefully. You may be able to see the usual insect traits—one pair of feelers, three pairs of legs attached to the chest or thorax, and three body divisions: head, thorax, and abdomen. You will notice, however, that springtails lack wings. You may also discover that some are hairy but others are covered with scales.

Insects' metabolic rates respond to the cold by slowing down. This causes the insect, at any stage in its development, to become dormant. There are two forms of dormancy: quiescence and diapause. Quiescence is a short-term event in which the insect responds to temporary changes in weather conditions. Diapause is a long-term dormancy. It is an overwintering strategy controlled by both daylight and temperature, though light seems to be the critical variable. During diapause, the insect remains in a state of lowered metabolic activity, until days lengthen and there is enough light to trigger hormonal activity, causing the insect to awaken. Different species of insects enter diapause as eggs, larvae, pupae, or adults.

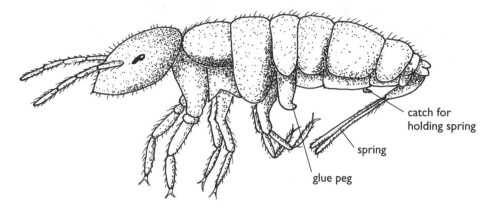

Springtails (Collembola) live in the surface layer of soil and leaf litter.

You can find out how quiescence works with some help from an ant, a bug box or other container, and a refrigerator. This experiment must be done when ants are still active.

1. Capture an ant in the container. Determine the temperature inside the refrigerator and record it in a notebook.

2. Put the container with the ant into the refrigerator. How long does it take for the ant to cease movement and become quiescent?

3. After you take the container out of the refrigerator, how long does it take the ant to resume its normal activity? Would a change in the cooling temperature (in the freezer, or longer in the refrigerator) affect the behavior of the ant? Try it.

4. Compare the amount of time one insect requires to recover from various temperature intervals with that of others of the same species.

5. You can try this investigation with other insects that use quiescent strategies, such as crickets, roaches, or termites. Compare your results for different species.

Capture Insects in the Soil

Many insects overwinter in the soil and in plant material, where they find a safe haven from the cold and from predators. If snow does not completely cover the ground or is not too deep, you can find some of these insects to examine. You will need a trowel for digging and a bucket to hold the soil. A Berlese funnel, or insect strainer, is an effective tool for capturing insects that live in the soil or in decaying leaves. You need a twenty-five- to seventy-five-watt bulb, a wide-mouth funnel (you can make one from aluminum foil), some wire screening, a quart-size wide-mouth jar, and enough rubbing alcohol to fill the jar to a level of about one-and-a-half to two inches. If you do not want to kill the insects, use water instead of the alcohol. (Some people add a thin layer of kerosene to prevent the alcohol from evaporating.)

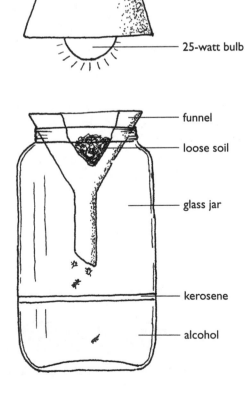

25-watt bulb

funnel

loose soil

glass jar

kerosene

alcohol

Berlese funnel

1. Cover the opening of the funnel with wire screening and put the funnel in the mouth of the jar.
2. Pour in a handful, or about a half cup, of loosely packed soil or leaf litter. You may have to fluff the soil or litter a little or let it dry out somewhat if it is wet.
3. Put the light source above the funnel to further dry out the soil. The insects in the soil will move down the funnel away from the heat toward moisture and tumble into the alcohol.
4. Keep the light on for about six hours. If you don't find any insects, try again with soil from another place. Beneath a tree is a good place to find soil that contains insects.
5. Examine the insects you have collected. How many different kinds did you trap? Do any have wings? Legs? How many? Do any of the insects look familiar to you? If you want to know what kind of insects they are, take your sample to a local nature center or your teacher for help in identifying them.
6. Repeat the procedure with samples of soil and leaf litter from different places, such as a wooded area, a field, and your backyard garden. Keep records of the insects you collect and where you found them.

Learn More about Winter Birds

Winter backyard birding has been going on for a long time. You can join the group by putting a bird feeder in your yard. The array of commercially available bird feeders can be confusing, because feeders come in a variety of styles and sizes.

Tube feeders with large plastic domes are useful for feeding a variety of birds. The dome does a pretty good job of thwarting squirrels and it keeps the seed dry. Another favorite is the platform feeder. These are easy to build and allow a large number of birds to gather for a meal. Don't forget to clean your feeder regularly. A soapy scrub and a good rinse will do the job.

You can make your own feeder from a two- or three-liter soda bottle and an inexpensive fitting designed especially for this kind of

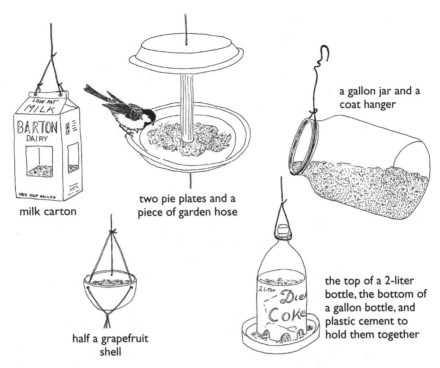

milk carton

two pie plates and a
piece of garden hose

a gallon jar and a
coat hanger

half a grapefruit
shell

the top of a 2-liter
bottle, the bottom of
a gallon bottle, and
plastic cement to
hold them together

Easy bird feeders

feeder, available at stores that sell bird feeders. The illustrations below show other types of low-cost feeders you can create to supply food for hungry birds.

Many birders are fascinated with one kind of bird or group of birds and have made extensive studies of them. Is there a particular type of bird visiting your feeder that you would like to know more about? You can begin a study of this bird by observing its behavior and recording your observations in a notebook.

1. At what time of the day does the bird come to the feeder? Is it a solitary feeder or does it feed with other birds? Does the bird feed only with its own kind or does it feed with other kinds of birds? Does it eat the seed while at the feeder or does it take the seed and fly away? If it eats at the feeder, how does it open the seed? What other behaviors do you observe? While making your observations, you will probably answer some questions of your own. Record these in your field notebook.

2. Another step in learning about your bird of choice is to read about it. There are many fine books devoted to one kind of bird, and you can find these at your local library or obtain them through the interlibrary loan system. The staff at a local bird sanctuary or members of a local bird group also may be able to help you.

3. When you have finished your research, write up a story about this bird that includes what you have learned. You may find that your local newspaper welcomes such stories about local birds written by a reader. A project such as this is fun to do with a friend. The following are some birds whose behavior you might like to explore.

4. **Nuthatches.** A suet feeder attached to a tree trunk will attract these small birds. Watch them for some fascinating behavior. Write a description of the bird as it works its way down the tree trunk. How does it hold its tail? Does it use the tail for support? How does it use its feet to prevent itself from tumbling to the ground?

5. **Woodpeckers.** Suet will also attract woodpeckers. Hairy and downy woodpeckers are frequent visitors to my suet cakes. You

White-breasted nuthatch   *Downy woodpecker*

American goldfinch

will need your guidebook to help you figure out which is which between these two very similar birds. Which has the longer bill? How do these birds use their tails when eating from the suet or digging insects from the tree bark? How do their feet differ from those of the perching birds? What is the advantage of this design?

6. **Goldfinches.** The goldfinches at your winter feeder are not dressed in the bright yellow of spring. Use your field guide to determine whether the bird is a male or a female. If it is a male, when will he molt and get his bright-colored feathers? Do goldfinches feed in groups of other birds or are they solitary birds that prefer to eat alone?

Identify Mammal Tracks

Winter is a time of hardship for most mammals. Food is scarce. Icy winds howl, snow falls, and the thermometer dips below freezing. Mammals that live in the wild do not have access to the technology we do, and cannot simply turn up the thermostat or go to the supermarket to stock up on supplies. In deep snow and bitter cold, they either survive or perish. They must rely on evolved strategies, but many of them die. Among black bears (Ursus americanus), however, there is an extremely good survival rate; only 1 or 2 percent of these shy, reclusive mammals die in any ordinary winter. How the bears manage the winter months has been the subject of scientific investigation for many years. These studies have revealed that black bears have developed complex strategies for coping with the cold season.

Many mammals remain hidden in dens, burrows, or tree cavities during the most severe periods of the winter. Those that do wander in search of food do so in the shadowy predawn hours or at dusk. The dim light coupled with the protective coloration of the animals' fur hides them from all but the sharpest eyes.

Although we usually do not see these animals, we can learn of their presence through the signatures they leave on the snow-covered landscape. The paws and hooves of animals make impressions in the snow, known as tracks, or prints. A series of prints makes a trail. Other signatures include droppings, or scat, toothmarks left on broken twigs, and clawmarks on the bark of trees. These visible clues alert us to the presence of the very shy mammals that are active in our neighborhoods throughout the winter. In the following activities, you will have an opportunity to peek into the private lives of those animals.

When mammals travel in the snow, they leave a series of prints. These prints, or tracks, provide us with some information about that animal: the direction in which it is going, what it may have been doing, whether it was traveling alone or with others of its own kind. We can sometimes also see from where the tracks lead whether the animal browsed on vegetation or left clawmarks on tree trunks.

The chart on the next page will help you focus on some of the characteristics of tracks and trails.

ANIMAL TRACKS

Mammal	Prints	Facts
Deer		
Dog		
Cat		
Eastern cottontail		
Gray squirrel		
Striped skunk		
Raccoon		
Opossum		

The length and width of a track are clues to help you decide which animal made the print. Different books use different measuring techniques, so if you are using a tracking book as a guide, you need to make sure you are measuring the tracks using the same method as described in the guide.

When taking measurements of prints, you will need to measure more than one track. After snow has fallen, it is affected by the environment, and prints or tracks made in it will change in appearance. Those you find in freshly fallen snow will look very different from those you find in slushy snow. You can discover this for yourself by making some footprints of your own in freshly fallen snow. Examine your prints the next day. How have they changed?

Keep a record of the animal tracks and trails you find in your neighborhood. Include a drawing, the date, weather conditions, time of day, type of animal, and comments.

6

IN THE WEATHER

Present the Tumbler Trick

In visualizing atmospheric pressure, imagine a column of air extending from a certain level up through the entire height of the atmosphere. Though this imaginary column has no walls, the concept helps us understand atmospheric pressure as the weight of all the air above that level. The weight is the total mass of all the air in the column, where the number of molecules in the thin air of the upper atmosphere is far less per unit volume than the number in compressed air at the surface. The higher you go, the less air there is above you, the less the weight per unit area, hence the less air pressure.

Pressure is not the result of the density of air alone, however. The pressure of a contained gas can be increased by adding heat. The opposite is also true; for example, if we put an inflated balloon in the refrigerator, its size shrinks because its internal pressure decreases. As air warms, it also expands, taking up more room with the same amount of air molecules, which decreases its density. Generally speaking, lower pressure areas are associated with cloudiness, precipitation, and storms, and higher pressure areas with fair weather and clearer skies.

Atmospheric pressure is exerted by the density of the gases in the air, and is not dependent on the orientation of the surface upon which it acts. The surface can even be upside down, as this activity so forcefully demonstrates. Here's a surprising way to observe air pressure without the use of measuring instruments.

1. Fill a drinking cup to the brim with water.
2. Place an index card on top of the cup's rim, making sure it covers the entire surface of the rim.
3. Pick up the cup and carefully turn it upside down. The air pressure outside the cup—greater than the water pressure inside the cup—holds the water in its place.

Make a Water Barometer

The force exerted by the atmosphere on the surface of the earth varies with the amount of air above it. More air above means higher pressure at the surface; less air means less pressure. A barometer reacts to the weight of the air above it and detects changes in pressure, which are associated with changes in the weather. Measure changes in atmospheric pressure with a simple barometer.

1. Obtain a plastic water bottle with screw-on lid and straw. Tightly screw the lid onto the bottle, with the straw extended about eight inches. Use a small bit of plasticene clay to seal the lid around the straw to make it completely airtight.
2. Put some water in a shallow bowl and add a little food coloring.
3. Turn the bottle upside down and insert the tip of the straw into the water. Slightly squeeze the bottle until a few bubbles rise through the water, and the water rises about halfway up the straw. Tape the water bottle to an inside corner to hold it in place.
4. Fold an index card in half lengthwise and tape it to the back of the straw.
5. Use pliers to squeeze the longer loop of a paper clip into a sharp angle to use as a pointer, and clip it to the card to mark the height of the water column in the straw.
6. Compare the change in height of the water in the tube every day. How does it correlate to the weather?

Make an Earth-o-meter

The earth makes one complete rotation on its axis per day. This is what makes the sun appear to move across the sky. With this homemade gadget, you can measure the speed of earth's rotation and compute the length of the day.

1. Pick a sunny location outside, and tape the handle of a magnifying lens on a chair so that the lens extends horizontally over the edge of the seat.
2. Place a piece of cardboard under the lens where the sun will shine through.
3. Raise the chair or the cardboard until a focused image of the sun appears on the cardboard and prop them in place.
4. Trace the focused image on the cardboard with a pencil.
5. Use a stop watch to measure the time in seconds it takes for the image to entirely leave the circle you've drawn.
6. Because the sun's diameter in the sky is approximately half a degree, in the amount of time it takes for its image to move out of the circle, the earth has rotated one half of 1 degree of its 360-degree rotation. Multiply your time by 720 to calculate the length of earth's day, in seconds. How close did you come to the solar day of 86,400 seconds? You can convert the seconds to minutes, then the minutes to hours, to see how close you came to the normal day of 24 hours.

Measure the Sun's Heat

Radiation is simply the transfer of energy that comes by the rapid oscillations of an electromagnetic field in space. Heat energy supplied by the sun's radiation is called insolation. The term comes from the words incoming solar radiation, and must not be confused with insulation, referring to materials that do not readily conduct heat or electricity.

Overall, the atmosphere loses heat while the earth's surface, except near the poles, gains it. In order to keep the tropics from continually getting warmer and the poles from continually getting colder, energy is transferred from lower to higher latitudes. This horizontal heat exchange is conducted primarily through atmospheric circulations, ocean currents, and the release of latent heat through condensation of moisture carried poleward.

Whenever the air is locally heated to a point where it is warmer than the surrounding air, free convection occurs: The parcel of air becomes buoyant and begins to rise, much like a hot air balloon. As the parcel rises, the pressure about it decreases, and buoyant air expands and cools. As long as this air remains warmer than its surroundings, it will continue to rise and continue to transfer heat from lower regions to upper levels.

The earth's curved surface receives solar radiation at unequal angles and intensities, leading to the circulations of the wind. Land and water surfaces absorb and lose heat at slower rates than the air does. Here's a way for you to figure out the rates of heat absorbed and retained by an object. The rates depend on the relationship between the distance and angle of a heat source, coupled with the object's basic characteristics.

1. Tape five thermometers across a meter stick at 0, 25, 50, 75, and 100 cm. (You could also use a yardstick, with the thermometers at 0, 9, 18, 27, and 36 inches.) Do not cover the thermometer bulbs.
2. Lay the stick on a table, with the zero end next to a neck lamp with a 100-watt bulb. Adjust the lamp to point the light bulb at the thermometer taped at 0, and turn on the lamp.
3. Record the temperatures of each of the five thermometers at one-minute intervals for ten minutes.
4. Turn off the lamp, and record the temperatures of each at one-minute intervals as they cool for ten minutes.
5. Graph the temperatures of each thermometer versus time. How do the results relate to the climates of different latitudes? Of the hemisphere's seasons?
6. Repeat the experiment with the thermometer bulbs in cups of water at these same distances, then in cups of soil. Extend the heating and cooling periods to twenty minutes each, reading the temperatures every two minutes. How do these results compare with the heating and cooling of the air?

Create an Inversion

A temperature inversion is a condition in which temperature increases with height, and is basically stable. A layer of warm air over cold air acts as a lid to confine movement and mixing to the layer below. Lingering inversions over cities surrounded by mountains prevent pollutants from rising and dissipating in the wind, and can lead to smog. This striking demonstration shows how a temperature inversion can prevent vertical movements of air.

You will need an aquarium tank, ice cubes, a neck lamp with a 100-watt bulb, plastic wrap or glass cover, incense, and matches.

1. Place several ice cubes on the bottom of an empty aquarium tank.
2. Using a neck lamp with a 100-watt bulb, point the light into the aquarium. Wait four to five minutes.
3. Now light a piece of incense and blow it out so it smolders and produces smoke; place it in the center of the aquarium bottom.
4. Cover the aquarium top completely with plastic wrap or a piece of glass. Observe where the smoke layer settles. With the warm air at the top of the aquarium, representing a temperature inversion, the smoke is trapped below.

Trap Transpiration

The earth's enormous water circulation system, called the hydrologic cycle, is powered by the processes of evaporation, transpiration, sublimation, condensation, and precipitation. All involve the changing and distribution of water as it is transported about the globe.

Evaporation—the conversion of liquid to vapor—is the largest source of atmospheric moisture. Evaporation largely functions near the earth's surface where rivers, lakes, and oceans offer saturated sources to the air. Evaporation occurs whenever relatively dry air comes into contact with a relatively wet surface. Water molecules constantly transfer back and forth between liquid and vapor phases.

The hydrologic cycle

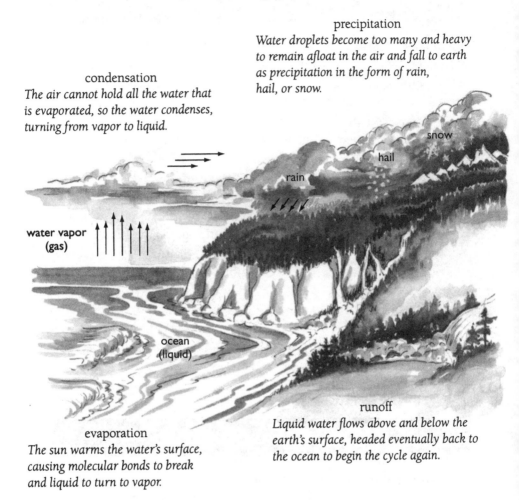

precipitation
Water droplets become too many and heavy to remain afloat in the air and fall to earth as precipitation in the form of rain, hail, or snow.

condensation
The air cannot hold all the water that is evaporated, so the water condenses, turning from vapor to liquid.

snow

hail

rain

water vapor
(gas)

ocean
(liquid)

runoff
Liquid water flows above and below the earth's surface, headed eventually back to the ocean to begin the cycle again.

evaporation
The sun warms the water's surface, causing molecular bonds to break and liquid to turn to vapor.

Water vapor sometimes changes directly into ice, without passing through the intermediate liquid state. This is called deposition, and is the process by which frost forms on winter windowpanes. The reverse process, from ice to vapor, is called sublimation. Sublimation is responsible for the way a snowbank may substantially diminish in strong sunshine without any noticeable melting.

Condensation occurs when water in the atmosphere changes from vapor to liquid or from liquid to ice. In doing so, it forms clouds, fog, dew, and frost, and can lead to precipitation. Condensation is also an important component of the energy balance, releasing the latent heat of water.

As water droplets or ice crystals grow in size, their falling velocity increases, and so does the tendency for growth through coalescing with other droplets or crystals. A typical raindrop is the end result of the coalition of upwards of one million cloud droplets. All water particles that eventually reach the ground are collectively called precipitation.

Transpiration, like evaporation, transfers moisture into the air, and refers to the contribution made by green growing plants. Groundwater absorbed from the soil is transported from the roots upward into the leaves. A chemical reaction involving solar radiation and the chlorophyll in the leaves releases water, and water vapor diffuses out of the plant and into the atmosphere.

Saturation of air results when the air can absorb no more water vapor. The intricate processes of transpiration and saturation are invisible. But here's a way for you to see them.

1. Place a wide-mouthed jar or glass upside down on a mowed lawn; wait a few minutes and observe the inside of the glass.
2. Moisture transpiring from the growing grass (and water evaporating from the soil) is continually added to the air under the glass. Soon the tiny atmosphere becomes saturated and cannot contain any more vapor. The excess condenses on the sides of the glass.
3. Try the procedure again on varying surfaces, such as soil, dry grass, or a potted flower to observe the results.
4. Try again under varying weather conditions: bright sunlight, overcast sky, cold and warm conditions. Record the elapsed time until droplets are observed. How does this rate of transpiration and/or evaporation vary with the weather conditions? With types of vegetation or ground cover?

Explore Evaporation

Spilled water disappears, wet clothes dry on a line, and sidewalk puddles vanish. The process responsible is called evaporation. Evaporation is the changing of liquid water to invisible water vapor, and it occurs through the action of heat. You can observe this happening by half filling two glasses with water.

1. Mark the level of the water in each glass with a fine-line marker. Place one glass on a windowsill, where the combined heat from the sun and the house heating system will cause evaporation to take place.
2. Place the second glass in a cool place away from sunlight. Leave both glasses in place for several days.
3. Make a mark on each glass that shows the water level each day. At the end of several days, what is the difference in the water level in the two glasses? Did the rate of evaporation vary according to where you put the glasses?

Make Dew

The dew point is the temperature at which the air becomes saturated (100 percent relative humidity) and excess moisture begins to condense, forming dew on exposed objects. If the dew point is at or below the freezing point of water, frost forms instead. You can force dew out of the air, and calculate the dew point.

1. Record the air temperature with a thermometer.
2. Nearly fill a metal can with water, making sure the outside of the can is dry.
3. Insert the thermometer into the water, and add ice, a little at a time, gently stirring with the thermometer. Because of the metal can's ability to readily conduct heat (or the lack of it), the air immediately surrounding the can cools to the same temperature as the water.

4. Observe the outside of the can; as soon as droplets form, record the temperature of the water, which is also the air's dew point.

5. While you cannot measure the dew point in the sky by this method, you can note the height at which it occurs by observing the flat bottoms of growing cumulus clouds. The rising, cooling air reaches its dew point at that altitude, the vapor begins to condense into droplets, and the cloud grows upward from that point. What can you deduce about how cloud base heights correspond to the relative humidity of the air and/or the temperature profiles above you?

Photograph the Weather

The most visible manifestation of the weather is the endlessly mutating variety of clouds. In their formation and development, their shapes and patterns, and their travel and distribution, we can find a more thorough understanding of the nature of the weather and its far-reaching influences.

Clouds come in an infinite variety of shapes, but a limited number of forms. Recognizing this, a basic cloud classification system was developed by the English pharmacist Luke Howard in 1803. Using Latin names to describe what he saw, his work remains the basis of today's system, with minor improvements: cumulus (a heap, pile, or mound) for convective clouds; stratus (spread or strewn) for layered clouds; cirrus (filament) for fibrous clouds; and nimbus (rain cloud) for storm clouds.

The never-ending sky panorama is an excellent subject for the art of photography. Because weather is constantly changing, a good photographer always has a camera handy. All the rules of good photography apply to create stunning sky scenes.

1. To start, take several shots of each cloud or sky subject: one at a regular setting, another a half-stop above, and a third at a half-stop below. Decide what exposure best suits your taste and objectives.

2. For each photo, record the date, time, location, camera direction, aperture, and speed, plus film type and film speed and filter type,

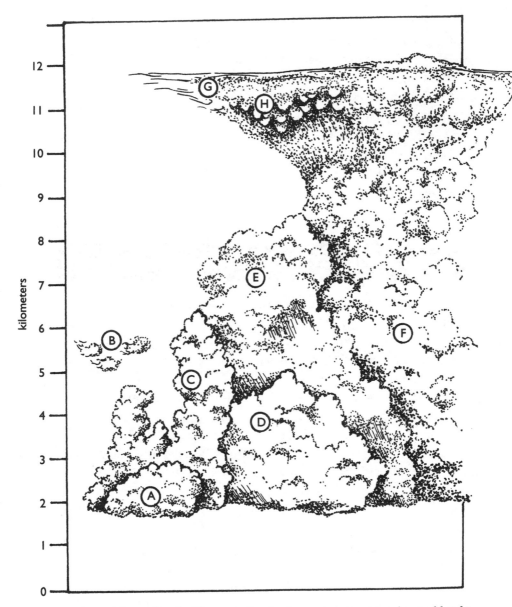

Cumuliform Clouds. *The vertical scale shows approximate and typical heights.*

a. *cumulus humilis (fair-weather cumulus)*
b. *cumulus floccus*
c. *cumulus castellanus*
d. *cumulus mediocris (towering cumulus)*

e. *cumulus congestus*
f. *cumulonimbus*
g. *anvil*
h. *mamma*

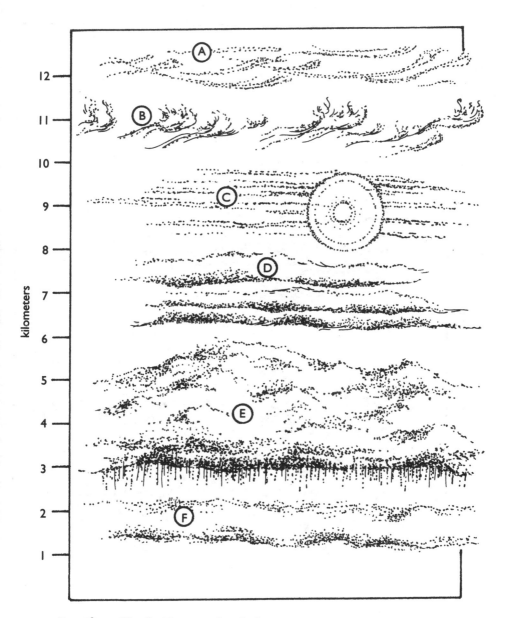

Stratiform Clouds. *The vertical scale shows approximate and typical heights.*

a. *cirrus*

b. *cirrus uncinus (mare's tails)*

c. *cirrostratus*

d. *altostratus*

e. *nimbostratus*

f. *stratus*

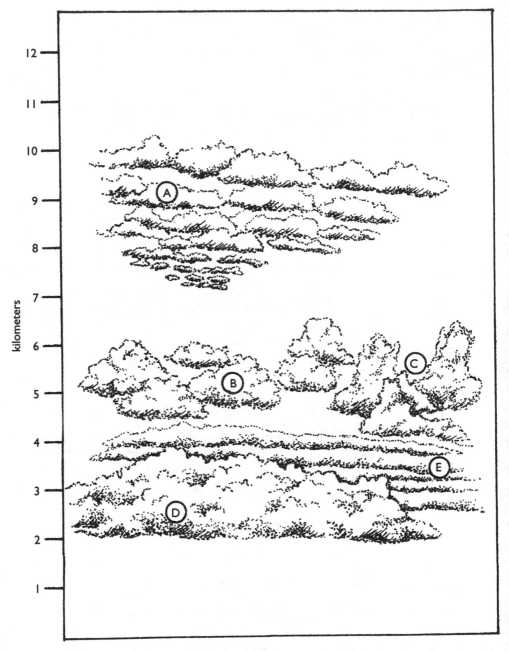

Duo-Process Clouds. *The vertical scale shows approximate and typical heights.*

a. cirrocumulus   c. altocumulus castellanus   e. stratocumulus undulatus
b. altocumulus   d. stratocumulus

as well as field notes of current weather, cloud type, heights, and direction of motion.

3. Make a cloud almanac. Capture specimens of several different types of clouds, and label them as cumulus, stratus, cirrus, and nimbus.
4. Try to photograph sunrises and sunsets. Be wary of overexposure.
5. Transfer collected specimens of snowflakes with a toothpick to chilled glass slides and shoot through a microscope lens.
6. Photographing lightning requires gambling with time exposures; work safely.
7. As with photographing lightning, use common sense when photographing storms and severe weather, and stay safe.
8. Shoot a series of time-lapse photographs such as the birth and death of a small cumulus cloud, the advance of a warm front, the full play of twilight, and other weather dramas.

Observe Updrafts and Falling Velocities

Millions of small-scale circulations and turbulent motions throughout the world form and dissipate each minute. Though small, these weather events are not insignificant, because they are both caused by and influence larger-scale patterns.

Chaotic motions that fluctuate wildly in seemingly random and unpredictable ways are called turbulence. Thermal turbulence is the sort caused by the rising air columns of convection. Mechanical turbulence is formed in airstreams roughed up by rugged terrain. Both types are involved in everyday observations: the random shape of clouds as they evolve; smoke dispersed by the wind; steam billowing from a cooling tower; the unpredictability of weather patterns themselves—all exhibit the influence of turbulence in the environment.

Lightning occurs during the explosive growth stage of a thunderstorm when a static charge builds up within the cloud as ice crystals and water droplets grow, interact, and collide. It is believed that the smaller particles tend to accumulate a positive charge near the top of the cloud, while larger ones that fall acquire a more negative charge.

The voltage difference between areas of opposite charges can reach up to 7,500 volts over the distance of just one inch, and millions of volts over the entire cloud! Once the voltage difference exceeds the insulating capacity of the air, a lightning stroke occurs to complete the electrical circuit and discharge the buildup of static electricity, marking the official transformation from rain cloud to thunderstorm.

Hailstones form when individual ice crystals at the tops of clouds remain for a time in an area of supercooled water droplets. This hailstone, in order to survive melting as it falls through the cloud and to the ground, must remain for at least a few minutes in the presence of supercooled water. This in turn requires updrafts strong enough to counteract the terminal fall velocity of the hailstone, typically 10 to 40 mph. Most thunderstorms do not develop such strong updrafts, and that is why hail that reaches the ground is relatively uncommon.

Updrafts in a cumulus cloud may rise at speeds of 15 to 30 feet per second, but may reach speeds of 125 to 200 feet per second, keeping raindrops and hailstones suspended in the air. As the raindrops or hailstones grow, they may eventually become too heavy to be supported by the updraft, and they fall out of the cloud. They reach terminal falling velocities according to their sizes, shapes, and weights. You can mimic an updraft that keeps raindrops or hailstones suspended.

1. Turn on a hair dryer and point it upward.
2. Place a Ping-Pong ball in its airstream. It will remain suspended in the flow.
3. If the hair dryer has different speeds, try each one.
4. Turn off the hair dryer, representing a cutoff in updraft.
5. Try again with a Nerf ball and a tennis ball. If the Nerf ball is too light, soak it in water and try again. What can you deduce about the sizes and weights of cloud droplets, raindrops, hailstones, and updrafts?
6. From a second-floor window, simultaneously drop all three balls. How does size, weight, density, and air resistance affect falling velocities?

Create "Lightning"

Lightning is a giant spark caused by the discharge of static electricity, as positive and negative electrical charges separate, build up, then suddenly jump from one location to another. It may occur between portions of the same cloud, from cloud to cloud, from cloud to ground, and from ground to cloud. Tiny sparks of static electricity mimic lightning strokes, but are harmless and easy to generate. You can get a charge out of some home-grown lightning made with static electricity. These experiments work best in dry air.

1. Rub a plastic comb with a piece of wool to charge the comb. Hold the comb near a metal doorknob and observe the spark it generates. Charge the comb again and insert it into a bowl of dry puffed rice; grains of rice stick to the comb. Bring the charged comb near a thin stream of water from a faucet; note how it deflects the flow.

2. Inflate a balloon and charge it by rubbing it against your hair; observe yourself in the mirror as you hold the balloon near your hair. Charge the balloon again with your hair or the wool and hold it over some pepper sprinkled on a plate. What happens? Add water to the plate and float some pepper on its surface. Bring the charged balloon near the water. What happens now?

3. Hang two inflated balloons side by side from a yardstick suspended between two chairs. Rub one with the wool. How do the balloons react? Rub both balloons to charge them equally: now what happens? Note that identical static electric charges repel each other; opposites attract.

4. Take off your shoes and shuffle across a carpeted room in your socks. Touch the doorknob or other metal object to discharge the static electricity that accumulated in your body.

5. Go into a darkened room and repeat the sock-shuffle shock experiment to better see the spark. Blow up two balloons, charge them with the wool, and touch them together in the dark. Observe your mini-lightning strikes. Pop the balloons to create thunder.

Dissect a Hailstone

The concentric rings of a hailstone give an indication of the number of times the hailstone crossed the freezing/melting level in the thunderstorm. Alternate layers of rime and glaze create the pattern. Splitting open a hailstone's interior reveals its formation of concentric layers of ice.

1. Collect hailstone specimens as soon as possible after they've landed.
2. Measure and record the diameters, circumferences, and weights, as well as the date, time, and location collected.
3. Spread them on the newspaper and use a hammer and chisel to split them apart.
4. Count the number of rings. Make sketches of them.

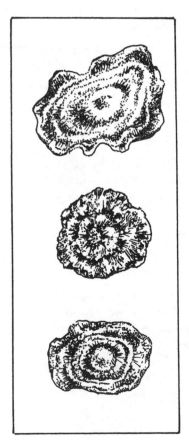

Cross Sections of Hailstones.
The concentric pattern is formed by alternating layers of rime and glaze as the hailstone revisits both sides of the freezing/melting level in its ride through the thunderstorm.

Follow the Snow

The definition of a snowstorm varies from place to place and can be applied to widely disparate storms, over a wide temperature range, in winds ranging from nearly calm to hurricane force. There is no difference in the physical structure of a snowstorm from that of a rainstorm; much of what falls as rain begins as snow in the upper levels. The only difference is the temperature profile in which the snow falls. In a snowstorm, the entire column tends to be at or below freezing, while in a raining or sleeting situation, air above freezing exists somewhere between the ground and the level at which the precipitation forms.

Snowstorms differ from other severe weather events in the extent and duration of their effects. Snow cover can last for an entire season, even though the storm may have visited for only a few hours. Once a large area is snow-covered, the overall albedo (reflectivity) of the region changes, reflecting more solar radiation back into space, reinforcing cold air at the surface, and maintaining a trough of lower pressure in the upper atmosphere—all of which is conducive to more snowstorms and greater snow accumulations.

For a snowstorm to produce heavy precipitation, there must be ample moisture in the air; and for that precipitation to be snow, it has to be cold at the cloud level. But to get those two conditions to mix in the same cloud at the same time is the trick. Air that is cold enough to make snow rarely contains much moisture. For heavy snow to fall, there must be a continual source of moisture feeding into the freezing air.

In many areas, snowfall accounts for a major portion of the region's total annual precipitation, providing important moisture during the growing season and for urban water use. A season's total snowfall may have a profound influence on agriculture and resource use, tourism and recreation, government, industry, and commerce. Observe and compile data on snowfall for an entire region during the cold season.

1. Keep a daily weather record of temperatures and precipitation types and amounts for an entire winter season using regional weather reports. Add your personal observations to others made in your region.

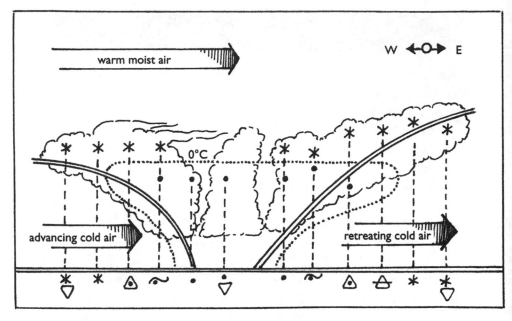

Winter precipitation varies depending on the temperature profile in which it forms.

2. Plot total recorded snowfalls on a regional map, and analyze the pattern.
3. Prepare another regional map with station observations of total precipitation, accounting for the water content of the snow, and analyze. How do the two maps compare?
4. Is there any indication of lake effect snow? Of upslope snow? Did the snowmelt cause any flooding? Were amounts adequate for expected needs? How did the snowfall affect the people of the region? How did this season compare to those in past years?

Make a Simple Psychrometer

By taking cues from the sky, trees, flowers, insects, and animals, from aching bunions and bones, and a thousand and one other indicators, one can make fairly accurate short-range forecasts. Observational forecasting requires a certain sensitivity to all of nature in all its forms—its sights, sounds, smells, textures, and even tastes. A simple, practical, and accurate assessment of what the weather is up to can be made by interpreting subtle causes and effects.

Measuring the air's moisture content can help you determine what kind of weather is headed your way. Hygrometers are the instruments used to measure the moisture content of the air. Since there are many ways to express it, there are almost as many types of hygrometers. A simple hygrometer that measures relative humidity is the psychrometer, consisting of a pair of thermometers, one of which has a piece of wetted cotton on its bulb. As water evaporates from the wet wick on the bulb, the air near its surface is cooled as the water absorbs heat from its surroundings to evaporate. The amount of evaporation depends on how much moisture is in the air already. At saturation, no more net evaporation into the air is possible, and the readings are equal for wet and dry bulbs; hence the relative humidity is 100 percent. At lesser humidity, the wet bulb will be at a lower temperature than the dry bulb.

If the moisture content in the air is high, you can prepare for rain. A simple rain gauge is a straight-sided cylinder, open at the top. Graduated markings etched or molded into the cylinder are used to measure the rainfall amount. Many rain gauges consist of a funnel on the top of a cylindrical can, which is partly sunk into the ground. The precipitation that falls through the opening is funneled into a smaller cylinder inside the larger one. This narrow inner can is sufficient for most rainfalls, but if it isn't, and overflows, the excess is still contained by the larger cylinder. Measurements are made to the nearest hundredth of an inch.

Water in the wick of a wet bulb thermometer absorbs heat from the surrounding air to evaporate, which is measured as a lower wet bulb temperature. The difference between the wet bulb and the dry bulb temperatures is used to determine the relative humidity of the air. Measure the relative humidity with a homemade psychrometer.

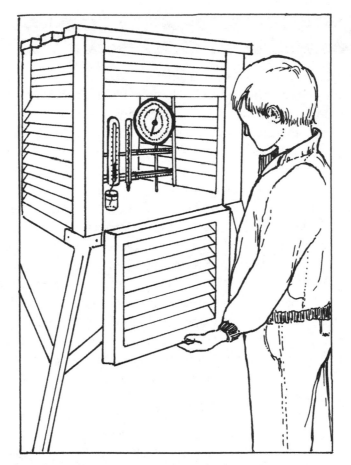

Weather Instrument Shelter. *A louvered instrument shelter allows ambient conditions to exist inside, while sun, wind, and precipitation are excluded. A fully equipped shelter may contain an aneroid barometer, minimum and maximum thermometers, and wet and dry bulb thermometers.*

1. Check the readings of two thermometers to be sure they agree. Mount them side by side.
2. Cut a shoelace to a length of about four inches or so; slip one end on one of the thermometer bulbs, and tie it on with thread. Put the other end of the shoelace into the small jar of water; it will act as a wick to keep the bulb wet.
3. Once the temperature of the wet bulb stabilizes, read both dry bulb and wet bulb thermometers; consult the accompanying relative humidity table to determine the relative humidity.

PSYCHROMETRIC TABLE FOR RELATIVE HUMIDITY

DRY BULB TEMPERATURE °F

RELATIVE HUMIDITY

WET BULB °F	40	42	44	46	48	50	52	54	56	58	60	62	64	66	68	70	72	74	76	78	80	82	84	86	88	90
30	24	14	6																							
32	38	28	18	10	3																					
34	53	41	31	22	14	7	1																			
36	68	55	44	34	25	17	10	2																		
38	84	70	57	46	36	28	20	14	8	3																
40	100	85	71	59	48	39	31	23	17	11	6	2														
42		100	85	72	60	50	41	33	26	20	14	10	5	2												
44			100	86	73	62	52	43	35	29	23	17	12	8	5	1										
46				100	86	74	63	54	45	38	31	25	20	15	11	7	4	1								
48					100	87	75	65	55	47	40	33	27	22	18	14	10	7	4	1						
50						100	87	76	66	57	49	42	35	30	24	20	16	12	9	6	4	2				
52							100	88	77	67	58	50	43	37	32	27	22	18	15	11	9	6	4	2		
54								100	88	78	68	60	52	45	39	33	29	24	20	17	14	11	8	6	4	2
56									100	89	78	69	61	53	47	41	35	30	26	22	19	16	13	10	8	6
58										100	89	79	70	62	55	48	42	37	32	28	24	21	17	15	12	10
60											100	89	80	71	63	56	50	44	38	34	30	26	22	19	16	14
62												100	90	80	72	64	57	51	45	40	35	31	27	24	21	18
64													100	90	81	72	65	58	52	46	41	37	33	29	25	22
66														100	90	81	73	66	59	53	48	43	38	34	30	27
68															100	90	82	74	67	60	54	49	44	39	35	32
70																100	91	82	74	67	61	55	50	45	41	37
72																	100	91	83	75	68	62	56	51	46	42
74																		100	91	83	76	69	63	57	52	47
76																			100	91	83	76	70	63	58	53
78																				100	91	84	77	70	64	59
80																					100	92	84	77	71	65
82																						100	92	84	78	71
84																							100	92	85	78

WET BULB TEMPERATURE °F

Catch Raindrops

Rainfall distribution patterns and amounts are determined from a network of rain gauges. Raindrop sizes and densities determine rainfall intensity. Make simple rain gauges and measure raindrop sizes.

1. Set several straight-sided cans out in the rain at various locations.
2. Use a plastic ruler marked in 32nds of an inch as a measuring stick. You may need to trim the end of the ruler so that the bottom is the zero point.
3. With these simple rain gauges, study local precipitation patterns. How do rainfall totals vary near buildings or trees or in the garden? How does the wind direction affect the amount collected in various gauges? Over a season, what wind direction brings the most rainfall? The least? The most intense?
4. Briefly set a shallow pan of flour out in the rain. Measure the diameters of the flour-coated drops. What is the range of sizes? How do sizes vary with the storm duration, intensity, and total rainfall?

Measure the Acidity of Rainwater

Complex chemical reactions in the air produce acidic compounds as pollutants combine with atmospheric moisture and gases. Pollution from motor vehicles and coal-fired power plants account for the three most common and serious acids: sulfur dioxides, nitrogen oxides, and volatile organic carbons. Acid rain occurs when these compounds are taken from the air by rainfall. It is thought that many pollutants interact in such a way to be more harmful as a group than individually. In severely affected areas, buildings, statues, gravestones, and other exposed structures and materials erode at alarming rates. Lakes may be devoid of life, soil nutrients depleted, and field crops stunted.

Global warming is also a serious problem that today's society faces. We still don't know whether the detected temperature increases in the global climate are the result of human activities or of natural causes.

Atmospheric nitrogen and oxygen, which make up 98 percent of the air, absorb virtually no infrared radiation from the sun, allowing it to escape to space. Water vapor and carbon dioxide, however, do absorb the radiation. The increasing concentrations of carbon dioxide—and other heat-absorbing gases such as methane, nitrous oxide, and CFCs—tend to raise the temperature, and are blamed on such human activities as burning fossil fuels, clear-cutting rain forests, and raising cattle and rice. On the other hand, the presence of sulfur dioxide in the atmosphere from power plants tends to increase cloud cover, which contributes to cooling.

The pH (potential of hydrogen) is a measure of the degree of acidity of a solution. Based on a 14-point scale, with 7 as neutral, solutions with a pH below 7 are acidic and those above 7 are basic, or alkaline. The scale is logarithmic, which means there is a tenfold difference between the whole numbers. A solution that has a pH of 2 is ten times more acidic than one of 3 and one hundred times as acidic as one with 4. Rainwater can be tested to determine how acidic or alkaline it is, and the result used to judge its effects on living organisms.

You will need some pH indicator test paper strips, a rain gauge, a small clean plastic or glass container, a pencil, and a piece of paper.

1. Place a small sample of collected rainwater in a small clean plastic or glass container and dip a one-inch-long strip of pH indicator paper in it. Compare the color of the test strip to the color chart and record the pH.

2. During the passage of a long-lasting storm, measure the pH at regular intervals. Does it change with time?

3. Collect some snow, let it melt, and measure its pH. Does the pH of snow change with the depth of your sample? Is there a pattern to the pH of precipitation over the course of the year?

4. Test the pH of a nearby pond, lake, or stream. How can this be affected by a sudden spring melt of acidic snow deposited earlier? How would a limestone soil or streambed affect the results of acid deposition?

Use Less Energy

Global warming may be the effect of human activity, although such theories are not certain. To determine how your family uses energy, keep a daily log of energy use to observe daily and seasonal variations.

1. Make daily readings of your gas and electric meters, and relate them to specific uses. Estimate the energy used in a hot shower versus a hot bath.

2. Record the amounts and costs of all fuels, and their total energy supply. Divide by the number of people in your household. How does your consumption compare with the local or national average?

3. Try some conservation measures: Add more insulation in the house, lower the thermostat, use public transportation, turn off unused appliances and lights, use a clothesline instead of a dryer, reuse and recycle products. You might also plant a row of trees as a windbreak for your house, compost food and vegetative wastes, stop fertilizing your lawn, or plant a vegetable garden to meet your own food requirements.

4. Consider installing some method of solar heating in your home, or purchase energy-efficient light bulbs.

5. Ride a bike to your destination instead of taking a car. You will not only lower pollution in the air, you will get great exercise!

7

IN ROCKS AND WATER

Grow Crystals

More than twenty-five hundred types of minerals have been discovered on earth. Although their variety of shapes appears numberless, they actually fall into six basic categories of shapes, or crystal systems. Minerals crystallize, or grow, from liquid solutions, beginning with their central cores and building outward. In the mineral quartz, for example, atoms fill a hexagonal structure that joins with other, similar structures as it grows into a larger, six-sided crystal. Quartz is therefore assigned to the hexagonal crystal system, and it is often found in rocks as masses of hexagonal crystals.

Toy and hobby stores sell crystal gardens to grow, but crystals also may be grown without a kit. Growing crystals requires a small amount of rock salt, which is usually stocked in supermarkets near ordinary table salt.

1. Fill a measuring cup with hot water.
2. Add two tablespoons of rock salt and stir the solution until the salt is dissolved.

3. Tie a piece of string around a pencil; rest the pencil across the top of the cup so that a length of string dangles into the salt water. Leave this crystal solution in a sunny place.

4. Note the changes in solution and on the string over the course of days and weeks. Sketch your observations and describe changes in the solution as the crystals grow.

Discover Mineral Cleavage

When a mineral breaks, it usually splits along layers of weakness called cleavage planes. The cleavage planes may be between layers of atoms or in planes where atomic bonds are weak. A salt crystal, consisting of alternating rows of sodium and chlorine atoms, breaks neatly in perfect cleavage planes between the rows. Micas, which are platy, flaky minerals common in many types of rocks, have perfect cleavage between the layers, in thin sheets parallel to the mineral's base. This simple activity illustrates how cleavage works in minerals.

1. Rip a six- to eight-inch-wide strip of cotton shirt or bedsheet fabric in the direction that is easiest to tear.

2. Cut the strip into six- to eight-inch squares. Two edges of the fabric will be cut and two edges torn.

3. Inspect the pieces of material with your hand lens. Can you see a pattern in the thread structure? Sketch the pattern in your notebook. Note on your sketch how the thread structure relates to the edges of the fabric.

4. Try to tear the fabric, first beginning at the torn edge, then beginning at the cut edge. Note your observations. Which direction was easier to tear? Think about the results of the tearing exercise and how other fabrics tear. What happens when you tear a hole in your pants or shirt? Does the cloth rip or tear in one direction? Two directions? All directions?

5. Next, inspect a paper towel. Using your hand lens, carefully observe the pattern in the paper towel created during its manufacture. Describe and sketch your observations in your notebook.

6. Try to tear the paper towel, first beginning at the perforated edge, then beginning at the finished edge. Which direction was easier to tear? Note any sensations or sounds. Write down any similarities or differences between tearing the fabric and the paper towel.

Create Cardboard Crystals

In this experiment, you can fold your own crystal shapes to create all six crystal systems.

1. Trace the crystal patterns on the next page onto tracing paper; add striations or markings as desired.
2. Tape the traced patterns onto thin cardboard and cut out the shapes.
3. Fold along the lines drawn, and fasten the edges with tape. You now have six crystal models, each representative of one crystal system.
4. Sketch the shapes. If you wish to create varieties of any one shape, experiment—add new features. You can copy nature by creating variations in each system: cubic (isometric), tetragonal, ortho-rhombic, monoclinic, triclinic, or hexagonal.
5. Next, place a protractor on a flat surface (desk or tabletop) with the straight measuring side closest to you.
6. Cross a ruler over the protractor, with an edge lined up on both the protractor's center dot (on the flat measuring side) and the 90-degree mark (on the curved measuring side). The ruler is now lying at a 90-degree angle to the straight measuring side of the protractor.
7. Place one side of the cubic (isometric) crystal model against the plastic ruler edge and one side against the flat measuring side of the protractor. Because the sides of the model line up with the ruler and protractor edges, the angles you are measuring on the cubic crystal are said to be 90-degree angles.
8. Measure each crystal model the same way. Do they all have 90-degree angles, or do you have to move the ruler to other degree marks on the protractor? Determine what angles each crystal has and write the numbers in your notebook.

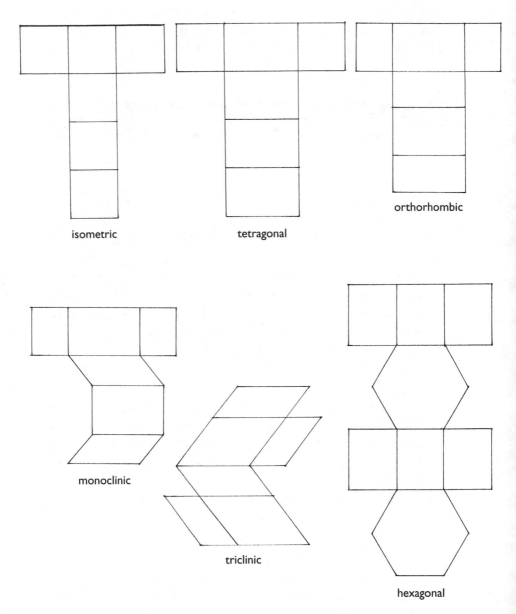

isometric

tetragonal

orthorhombic

monoclinic

triclinic

hexagonal

The six basic shapes of crystals

Make Edible Crystals

This experiment illustrates atomic structures within crystalline shapes.

1. Using miniature marshmallows and toothpicks, how would you begin to build a square? A cube? Try it.
2. Using eight marshmallows and twelve toothpicks, build a model of a cubic (isometric) crystal.
3. Using eight more marshmallows and twelve more toothpicks, build a tetragonal crystal structure. Will all the toothpicks for this model be the same length, or will you have to break a few to shorten them?
4. Sketch the models before eating the marshmallows. How might you build an orthorhombic crystal model of marshmallows and toothpicks? A hexagonal model?

Examine Edible "Rocks"

Three types of rocks are found on earth: igneous, sedimentary, and metamorphic. Rocks are grouped by type according to the different earth processes that make them.

Igneous means "of fire." Most igneous rocks are masses of minerals that crystallize out of burning-hot liquids found deep in the earth. Igneous rocks are found as both underground, plutonic rocks and aboveground, volcanic rocks. Some common forms are granite, gabbro, basalt, and rhyolite.

Sedimentary rocks are made of particles that have been moved by wind and water and have come to rest in rivers, lakes, ponds, seas, sand dunes, deltas, and deserts. Over time, the particles have been cemented together. The particles, or sediments, that compose sedimentary rocks can be of all sizes, from submicroscopic to larger than a house, and include pebbles, sand, pieces of shell, microscopic mineral grains, silt, mud, and clay. Sedimentary rocks are also the rocks most likely to hold fossils, the remains of plants and animals that were buried as the sediments were deposited. Sandstone, shale, conglomerate, limestone, and coal are types of sedimentary rocks.

Four common igneous rocks

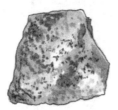

Granite is a pink or gray plutonic rock with medium to large mineral grains.

Domes, crags, spires, and castle shapes form in areas where large bodies of granite have been exposed by erosion. Half Dome in Yosemite National Park, California, is a granitic dome.

Gabbro is another plutonic rock with dark-colored minerals large enough to be visible without using a hand lens or microscope.

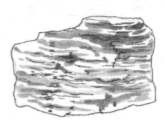

Rhyolite, a fine-grained volcanic rock, should be examined for flow lines, created when the magma is still hot and moving.

Basalt, a common igneous rock popularly known as lava, often forms in thick flows that cool and solidify into layers of rock broken into columns by vertical joints. Basalt columns like these in Devils Postpile National Monument, California, can be seen in many areas of past volcanic activity.

Samples of basalt may contain numerous cavities that formed when trapped gases escaped from the cooling magma.

Metamorphic rocks are altered igneous, sedimentary, or older meta-morphic rocks, products of high pressures, high temperatures, and chemical activity. Changes can be small, as when a layer of shale is squeezed under the weight of overlying sediment just enough to be compressed into slate, or great, as when the igneous rock granite par-tially remelts under heat and pressure to form a banded metamorphic rock known as gneiss. As a rock is altered or metamorphosed, its min-erals change their shapes and chemical makeups. Metamorphic rocks include shale, schist, gneiss, marble, and metaquartzite.

Three common sedimentary rocks

Sandstone is made of sand particles, often held together by sedimentary cement. Sandstone may be soft or hard depending on the composition of the cement.

Thick layers of sandstone can weather into landforms with many colors and shapes, especially in arid regions where the layers are well exposed. Formations like these can be seen in desert regions of Africa and the southwestern United States.

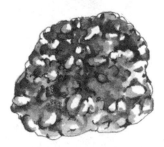

Shale consists of microscopic particles of silt and clay compacted into thin, hard layers parallel to sedimentary bedding. Shale tends to split along these layers.

Conglomerate has rounded particles that can range in size from pebbles to boulders held in a finer-grained material called the matrix.

Five common metamorphic rocks

Slate is metamorphosed shale and is easily split into thin sheets along parallel planes. Shiny flakes of mica may be visible on sheet surfaces.

Metaquartzite, an altered quartz-rich sandstone with a hardness around 7, has an uneven, often conchoidal fracture.

Schist is medium to coarse grained with distinct parallel mineral alignment from metamorphism by heat and pressure.

The intense folding displayed in layers of granular minerals in gneisses takes place deep in the earth's crust.

Pure marble, composed of only calcite or dolomite, is generally pure white. Other minerals act as coloring agents, adding spots or veinlike patterns known as marbling.

Marble, with a hardness of 3, can easily be scratched with a knife blade. For ages, sculptors have carved statues and ornaments of marble.

The rock cycle

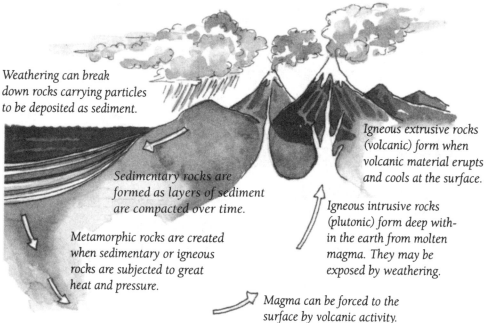

Weathering can break down rocks carrying particles to be deposited as sediment.

Igneous extrusive rocks (volcanic) form when volcanic material erupts and cools at the surface.

Sedimentary rocks are formed as layers of sediment are compacted over time.

Igneous intrusive rocks (plutonic) form deep within the earth from molten magma. They may be exposed by weathering.

Metamorphic rocks are created when sedimentary or igneous rocks are subjected to great heat and pressure.

Magma can be forced to the surface by volcanic activity.

With further heating, metamorphic rocks melt, becoming molten magma.

You can learn more about these types of rocks by consulting a field guide.

This edible "rock" experiment is best shared with friends. You will need various candies and cookies to examine.

1. Place each type of candy and cookie on a separate plate on a table. You may have, for example, brownies, chocolate chip cookies, malted milk balls, hard toffee, Rice Krispies treats, milk chocolate bars, and peanut butter cups, each on a different plate.

2. Describe each type of sweet as you would a rock: Does it have layers? What are the particle sizes? Is it hard or soft?

3. If you have asked friends or family members to help you with this exercise, give them each a pen and paper and ask them to record their impressions of each type. Use a field guide to associate the samples with real rock types.

4. Your conclusions might be something like this:
   - Hard toffee has conchoidal fracture like obsidian.
   - Chocolate chip cookies have scattered larger particles in a fine-grained mass, like garnet schist.
   - Rice Krispies treats have large pieces cemented together, like conglomerate.
5. Be creative while conducting your experiment! Then eat the "rocks."

Cook a Conglomerate

Conglomerate is a sedimentary rock composed of various-sized rock particles cemented together. You can bake your own conglomerate, which can be used in the experiment above. You will need a recipe for Rice Krispies treats and its ingredients, as well as rice puff and wheat puff cereal.

1. Follow the Rice Krispies treats recipe directions, but use one-third Rice Krispies, one-third wheat puffs, and one-third rice puffs instead of all Rice Krispies.
2. Once you have made the conglomeratic mixture, spread it into a baking pan.
3. After you have cooled the treats, note the appearance of the particles in size, shape, and color. Taste the treats to determine how the combination of flavors and textures are very different from original Rice Krispies treats.

Model Sedimentary Layers

Deposition, the laying down of sedimentary particles, is always at work on the earth's surface. Solid rock is constantly being torn down, only to have its pieces carried elsewhere. Wind, water, and gravity all serve as modes of transportation for sediment.

Two important geologic laws of deposition help us understand sedimentary rocks. The laws were proposed in 1669 by Danish physi-

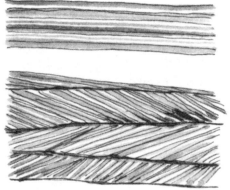

Steno's law of original horizontality states that sediments are deposited in horizontal layers parallel or nearly parallel to the ground.

Cross-bedding in sandstones forms at angles to bedding planes that are generally horizontal and parallel to the ground.

Steno's law of superposition states that younger sediments are deposited on top of older sediments. The bottom layer in this drawing, perhaps a massive unit of lime-stone, is probably the oldest. The stippled top layer, a sandstone, is probably younger than underlying layers, which grade from older to younger from bottom to top.

cian Niels Stensen, also known as Nicholas Steno. Steno's laws are rec-ognized today as important foundations of the science of geology.

The first is the law of original horizontality, which says that sedi-ments are deposited in horizontal layers, or beds, parallel or nearly parallel to ground surface. Certain sedimentary rocks, especially sand-stones, may show internal layering at an angle to the overall bed of rock.

The second of Steno's laws is the principle of superposition, which says that younger sedimentary beds are deposited on top of older beds. According to this principle, layers of sediments are arranged from older to younger, from bottom to top, in any sequence of deposited beds. If we apply Steno's laws with great care and intelligence, they serve well in our study of sedimentary rocks.

Heavy (large or dense) particles settle through water more readily than light (small or not dense) particles. If heavy and light particles are mixed in still water, the heavier particles will settle first, creating a bot-tom layer above which the lighter particles settle. The transition of heavy to light particles from bottom to top is called grading. You can make a model of sedimentary layers using materials from your kitchen and the grocery store.

You will need a clean glass jar with a lid, ¼ cup large dried lima beans, ¼ cup dried pinto beans, ¼ cup uncooked rice, and ¼ cup crushed cereal.

1. Place all the ingredients, one at a time, into a glass jar. The jar must be big enough to hold all the ingredients, water, and two inches of air below the lid.
2. Add water to the jar until the ingredients are covered. Screw the lid on securely and shake the jar.
3. Set the jar on a flat surface and do not disturb. Observe what happens to the ingredients in the jar. Record your observations beginning one minute after shaking.
4. Continue observing for fifteen minutes, recording observations at three-minute intervals. Note how long it takes the various particles to settle, which settle first, how they look as they settle, and how grain sizes change from layer to layer. Compare the number of layers with the number of ingredients used in preparing the experiment.

Dig Up Dirt

Soil is the relatively loose upper layer of earth that may be dug or plowed and in which plants grow. The upper dark layer of six to eight inches is topsoil, rich in humus, a dark material resulting from the decomposition of plants and animals. In some parts of the world, topsoil can be six feet deep. Below the topsoil lies the more compact and less fertile subsoil. It is lighter in color, not as rich in decomposed organic matter. Beneath the subsoil lies the parent material, the rock from which soil is derived—either broken rock or bedrock, the final and lowest layer any casual hole-digger can reach.

You can learn about layers of earth by digging a hole in the ground near your home.

1. In your garden or yard, dig a hole large enough to display the layers of earth beneath your feet. Make sure the hole is in a safe place so that no people or pets will fall in while you work.

2. While digging, notice changes in the ground's hardness as you go deeper. Measure the depth and width of your excavation with a measuring tape.
3. Sketch any changes in the earth's color and texture in a notebook. Note layers in the earthen sides of the hole, their thickness, whether the earth is wet or dry, whether there are pieces of broken rock, and when, if ever, you reach a thick layer of rock you cannot penetrate.
4. Using a hand lens, study samples of the different materials more closely.

Collect Sand

The color of beach sand depends on the color of its parent rock. In the United States, much of the beach sand is gray, composed of tiny particles of disintegrated granite. Some Florida beaches are expanses of white sand, made of minute bits of broken coral. Hawaii has black and green sand beaches of volcanic rock particles. Some black sand beaches are composed of tiny iron particles rather than bits of volcanic rock. Other clast (fragments from older rocks) colors you may observe in sand include light brown (pieces of granite or quartz), yellow (quartz), gold (mica), red (garnet), and pink (feldspar). If you look closely at the sand at the coast, river, or lake, you can analyze the type of rock from which the sand came.

1. Collect sand in small amounts from various beaches and sandboxes. Keep your sand samples separate by sealing them in plastic bags.
2. Label each bag with the date and location of sample collection.
3. Using a hand lens, look closely at each sample. Describe it in terms of color, roundness, and clast size. Guess what types of rock the particles came from.

Make a Chemical Volcano

Volcanoes often form when an oceanic plate bumps into a continental plate. There, the heavier, thinner crust of the seafloor dives beneath the continent, slides under it, and melts as the oceanic plate absorbs heat from the mantle. The dark rocks of oceanic plates are basalt, and as they melt and rise back to the earth's surface, they melt rocks from the continental crust as well. Depending on how much of the continental crust melts, different kinds of magmas result.

Shapes of volcanic mountains also vary. Thin, hot basaltic lavas in Hawaiian eruptions form gently sloping shield volcanoes, built by thousands of individual lava flows piled on top of each other. Shield volcanoes can build to great heights over many years. Alternating layers

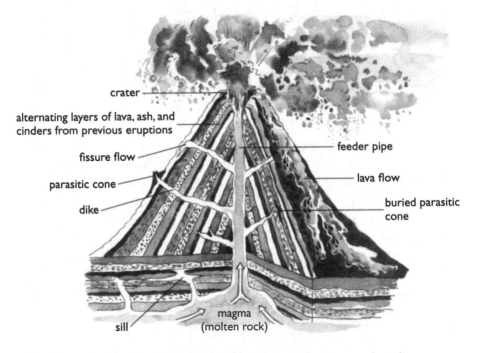

The shapes of volcanic mountains vary with rock type. Classic, cone-shaped volcanoes are called composite volcanoes, built of alternating layers of ash and lava. Within the volcano are feeder dikes and pipes, through which magma travels.

of ash and lava in varied eruptions build composite volcanoes, the classic volcanic cone shape. Ash or cinder cones result when an eruption is mainly explosive, or pyroclastic; loose material lies in a conical pile around the vent.

This experiment, best done outdoors, shows how the gas in a volcano pushes up and out through its small opening at the top. The baking soda, which is a base, and the vinegar, which is an acid, react together to release carbon dioxide, a gas. The carbon dioxide gas, which is heavier than air, pushes the mixture from the bottle. Adding detergent helps make more bubbles, simulating frothy, gas-charged lava, and food coloring creates a red-hot appearance.

1. Set a 25-ounce narrow-necked bottle on the ground and build a mound of soil up around it. Make the top of your mound about even with the bottle opening to keep the bottle as steady as possible. Shape the dirt to look like any volcano you wish: conical, shield, or composite. If you are unable to go outdoors, work in the sink—volcanic eruptions can be messy.
2. Pour one teaspoon of liquid dishwashing detergent into the bottle.
3. Add a few drops of red food coloring.
4. Add one cup of vinegar, then pour warm water almost to the top.
5. Very quickly add two teaspoons of soda mixed with a little water. Then watch the eruption.

Bake Volcano Tarts

A missing component in the chemical volcano experiment described above is heat. Baking volcano tarts shows how heat drives an eruption. As it heats up, the jam in the tart builds up pressure until it pours through the hole in the top of the crust. Similarly, a volcano is filled with hot magma that builds up pressure until it pours forth through its vent. In the previous experiment, we saw how the gas content within the magma increases its pressure. In this experiment, we see how heat increases the magma's pressure. In a real volcano, the combination of heat and gas brings on the pressure and eruption.

1. Preheat the oven to 375 degrees.
2. Take a package of pie crust dough and roll it out until thin and even.
3. Cut out circles with a knife or cookie cutter to the approximate size of the bowls in a muffin tin.
4. Put a circle of pie dough in the base of each muffin bowl, and spoon a teaspoon of raspberry jam on top.
5. Cover the jam with lids of dough, also cut into circles about the size of the muffin bowls.
6. Press down the edges to seal in the jam.
7. Poke a small hole in the center of each volcano tart with your knife.
8. Bake the tarts in the preheated oven. Note the changes after ten, twenty, and thirty minutes of baking.
9. Continue baking for about forty minutes or until the jam has erupted out of the tarts.
10. Pull them out of the oven and observe. How has the jam (magma) behaved in the various muffin bowls? Let the volcanic tarts cool before consuming.

Fracture Glass

If solids are not flexible, as glass is not, they can fracture when they expand. The hot rock in volcanoes and geysers usually heats the rocks near them, causing them to crack or break. The resulting fractures fill with magma. You can demonstrate how heat makes fractures by cooking marbles on your stove. Always use a hot pad when handling the tongs or skillet handle, and be sure to wear safety glasses.

1. Warm a heavy skillet over low heat on your stove.
2. Place a few glass marbles in the skillet, increase the heat, rolling the marbles occasionally with a pair of metal tongs. Watch how the heating affects the marbles.
3. Next, using the tongs, plunge each marble into a pot of ice water. Do they once again change in appearance, this time from quick cooling? Are the changes deep or on the surface?

Observe How Pumice Floats

Pumice, a type of volcanic rock, is light enough to float. Even though water enters some of the vesicles, or air holes, it cannot enter all the vesicles to sink the rock. To see how the air in pumice works to keep the rock afloat, try the following simple experiment.

1. Place a dry sponge in a sink with water.
2. Notice that the sponge floats, especially when dry, but even when wet. Where does the water go in a soaked sponge? If a sponge is getting wet and soggy, why does it still float?
3. You can also try this experiment with pumice sold at rock shops and hardware stores.

Make Soda Erupt

The thickness of a magma determines how explosive a volcanic eruption will be, but so does the magma's gas content. Two identical magmas will erupt differently if one has more trapped gases than the other. Inside a can of soda, carbon dioxide gas is trapped and cannot expand, as gases are trapped within a volcano that has not yet erupted. Experimenting with canned soda is easy and gives a good illustration of volcanic activity.

1. Give the can a good shake, then, holding the soda as far from you as possible, quickly pull the top open and watch what erupts.
2. Do you think warm soda will erupt more violently than cold soda? Will different sodas erupt differently?

Hunt for Fossils

For any animal or plant to become a fossil, it must be buried by sand, silt, mud, or other sediments in a river, lake, pond, swamp, or other environment. Although many organisms die and decompose on the ground before burial, others are covered first and protected from rotting when wind or water deposits sediment over the organism. If a plant or animal is buried soon after its death, its bony or wooden hard parts—bones, shells, teeth, branches—may be preserved in the enclosing sediments.

Body parts can be preserved in several ways. Burial may be quick enough or the organism's environment so hot and dry that a body is preserved nearly intact, both in its chemical composition and structure. Or the hard parts may petrify (turn to stone) when rainwater seeps into microscopic pores throughout the bone or wood, leaching away the original material and filling the tiny holes with harder minerals. Fossils also are preserved when a creature's body parts dissolve away completely after burial, leaving behind an empty mold in the rock. If the mold later fills with mineral matter carried by seeping rainwater, a fossil cast is made.

Searching for fossils requires little more than the proper field equipment and comfortable clothing. Rocks proven to contain fossils in the past may hold many more, still undiscovered. You have only to spot them. Remember that guidelines for finding fossils are only guidelines. Stay open-minded about what you might see in the field.

1. First identify your area of interest and decide where you want to go. Do you want to look at fossils of ancient shelled creatures, dinosaurs, or fernlike plants? Are you interested in a particular geologic time, such as the time of the woolly mammoths and other big mammals or the time when trilobites filled the seas?

2. Check a pocket guide for the age of fossils that interest you and the types of rock in which they are usually found. Also check your local library, museums, and bookstores. Often fossil specimens can be found near your home, if you know details about them before you set out. Compare the information you uncover from the above resources with a geologic map of your area.

A fossil brachiopod (lamp shell) from the Pennsylvanian period is shown embedded in limestone.

A similar brachiopod has eroded from the limestone that once held it.

A section of the stem of a fossil crinoid, or Pennsylvanian-age "sea lily," is shown as it once lived, attached by its stem to the ocean floor.

3. If you decide to fossil hunt on privately owned land, you must get permission from the landowner by telephoning or sending a letter. Even if the area is publicly owned, you need permission from the organization in charge if you plan to do more than look, draw, or photograph.

4. Once in the field, look for biological forms: ring shapes of shells, branching patterns of plants, cylindrical shapes of long shells, subtle imprints of feet, or animal burrows. Sketch what you find in a notebook, and pay close attention to the rocks as well as their fossils.

Observe How Bones Move

What happens to an organism between its time of death and time of burial affects how its fossils will appear. Fossil bones may not lie in the positions they assumed when the animal died. In this experiment, the toothpicks represent fossil bones, which may be carried off by scavenging animals, rolled on the bottom of a river, scattered in ocean currents, swept away in floods, or decomposed before burial.

1. Find a flat, smooth surface outdoors, exposed to wind and precipitation.
2. Set five or six toothpicks in an orderly pattern on the surface. Sketch the pattern in your field notebook. Note the time of day, weather, and wind direction. If you have pets that might disturb the toothpicks, good. Chance encounters with animals are part of the experiment.
3. Leave the toothpicks alone, but check them occasionally. Note the times and any changes in weather. If the toothpicks have moved, sketch a picture in your notebook and note what caused them to move.
4. After several days, draw a final picture of their pattern. Check to see how the pattern relates to prevailing wind or other environmental factors.

Look for Fossil Tracks

To become a fossil track, a footprint must be made in sediment that can take and hold an impression. The mud, sand, or silt should be moderately wet. If the sediments are dry, they may not be soft enough to imprint or they may blow away in the wind. The footprint must also be buried quickly, before it can crumble, to become a fossil. Most fossil footprints were probably made near or in water, where sediment quickly washed in to fill them. Animal tracks provide clues about how they may become trace fossils in the future.

1. As you go on hikes—in the woods, in parks, at the beach, in empty lots near your home—look for animals and their footprints. You may see an animal and then snoop around to find its tracks, or you can check the edges of puddles or ponds.
2. When you find some animal tracks, sketch them and identify them from guidebooks. Think about the tales the tracks tell. How wet was the mud when the tracks were made? Is it still that wet? How long ago do you think the animals came for water? How many different types of animals visited? Will the tracks eventually become fossils?

Make Molds and Casts of Tracks

Animals leave footprints that sometimes act as molds, filling with soil and sand that eventually harden into rocks. In this experiment, the original filling hardens into a cast. When the finished cast is set inside the milk carton and covered with plaster, the result is a mold that should closely resemble the original footprint.

1. Find a footprint to cast. Following the directions on a package of plaster of paris, mix the plaster in a plastic container.
2. Spoon the mixed plaster in a layer about one-inch thick over the footprint.
3. Let the mixture set for a few hours, until it is pretty hard. Then you can remove it from the ground and take it indoors overnight to harden completely. You will then have a cast of the footprint.
4. In the morning, brush the cast clean. Using a pocketknife to remove extra plaster, trim the cast to the size of a milk carton—cut in half to make a four-inch-high container—and set the cast inside, footprint side up.
5. Coat the top of the cast with a generous layer of dish soap. Let the soap seep down all along the sides of the cast.
6. Next, mix another batch of plaster. Spoon it in over the top of the cast. Let the mixture harden all day and overnight.
7. The next morning, tear away the milk carton and see what has happened. You should be able to pull apart the two halves—both cast and mold—of your plaster creation.

Understand Isostasy

Theories of continental movement date back as far as 1858, when writer Antonio Snider-Pellegrini, attempting to explain why fossils of identical animal species were found on widely separate continents, suggested that all the world's continents had once been joined in a single mass. In 1908, American geologist Frank Taylor theorized that the continents must be moving horizontally. He explained that great mountain ranges could result from slow continental collisions and even indicated a known line of undersea mountains between South America and Africa as the zone of separation or rifting of continents. Taylor named the mountains the Mid-Atlantic Ridge. Then, in 1912, German meteorologist Alfred Wegener observed that rock, fossil, and climatological evidence suggested that the continents had once been part of a single ancestral landmass. He named the mother continent Pangaea, meaning "all earth." Wegener suggested, as Taylor had, that the continents had drifted apart and continue to drift. Later, he became known as the father of the theory of continental drift.

One of geology's interesting principles is the theory of isostasy, which states that crustal plates of different sizes and densities will balance in the underlying mantle like icebergs in the ocean. Isostasy is achieved in part because of density differences between continental and oceanic crust and the underlying mantle. Continents rise above the floors of oceanic crust because they are composed of less-dense rocks. The following activity demonstrates the concept of isostasy.

1. Fill a 9 x 13 x 2–inch baking pan with water, and place two Styrofoam blocks of different sizes on the water. Sketch their appearance as they float side by side.

2. Scoop a few teaspoonfuls of sand onto one of the blocks. Note the changes in your notebook.

3. Next, scoop sand from the sandy block onto the other, and note how both readjust in the water. Your sketches of each stage of the experiment will help not only in your observations but also in answering questions about isostasy.

Reconstruct Pangaea

Scientists believe that the continents have maintained their present masses since around the beginning of the Paleozoic Era, between 750 and 550 million years ago, when the ancestral landmass, Pangaea, broke up. Where continents do not mesh exactly is where erosion probably has caused relatively minor changes in continental outlines. Early scientific thought with respect to continental drift was that the continents never could have traveled such huge distances without their shapes having been greatly altered by erosive forces. Now such forces are believed to be small compared with tectonic forces. Make a model of the world's most recent supercontinent using the puzzle pieces on the next page.

1. Trace the puzzle pieces onto a piece of paper.
2. Glue the pieces to the cardboard and let dry.
3. Cut out the puzzle pieces.
4. Arrange them into one large landmass. You can stop there, or you can go on and demonstrate other continental movements.
5. Move the puzzle pieces to simulate each stage in continental movement. Note any rift zones, mountain chains, and features that can be traced across oceans. Where are the gaps in coastlines, and why do they exist? Where are the poles and equator for each configuration of continents?

Create Convection Currents

The circulation of the earth's heat in patterns that drive the crustal plates on the mantle is known as convection, a process easily illustrated with water and food coloring. The water represents the mantle, and its flow in response to differences in temperature represents convection currents within the mantle. Think of the paper dots as crust, lighter material floating on denser moving material. Crustal plates are transported on denser mantle material in response to convection currents within the mantle. When currents reach the edge of their cycle, they dive down, forming circular patterns called convection cells.

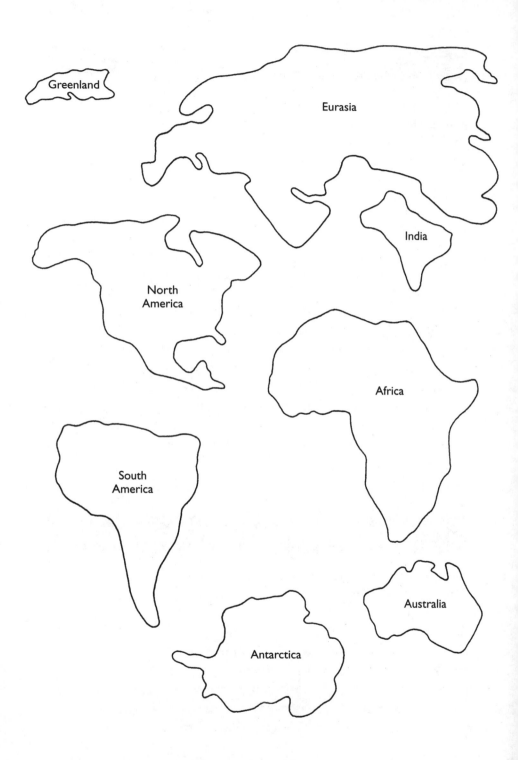

1. Fill a deep metal pan with water to within an inch of the top.
2. Place the left edge of the pan on a hot plate, propping up the over-hanging right edge with another pan or wooden blocks. Be sure to allow enough space around the hot plate to prevent fire danger.
3. Place a bag filled with ice cubes against the right side of the metal pan. Note that the pan will become partly hot and partly cold, so be sure to use oven mitts.
4. Use one eyedropper for blue food coloring and one for red. Drop three drops of blue into the water on the cold side and three drops of red on the hot side. Observe what happens to the colors, where they go when the currents reach the sides of the pan.
5. Carefully sprinkle paper dots made with a hole-puncher onto the water surface. Observe where they go and how they behave when they reach the edge of the pan.

Travel Fault Lines

Historical records since before the time of Christ describe great shaking of the ground, accounts interpreted by scholars to be descriptions of earthquakes. But not until the studies of 1906 did we recognize that earthquakes are caused by slippage along faults, or breaks in the earth's crust. Measurements taken before and after the occurrence of a San Francisco earthquake in 1906 indicated that the rocks near the San Andreas fault had been broken and offset.

From observations, Harry F. Reid of Johns Hopkins University came up with the elastic-rebound theory of earthquake generation. The theory states that rocks behave elastically—they are capable of recovering size and shape after being deformed or strained. When two rock masses on opposite sides of a fault strain in different directions, they cannot move because of friction, and energy is stored. When the energy builds up enough to overcome friction, the rocks break at their weakest point. They spring back to an equilibrium state. The elastic rebound, or springing back, releases energy in the form of heat generated by the movement and as earthquake, or seismic, waves.

Elastic rebound of the earth's crust

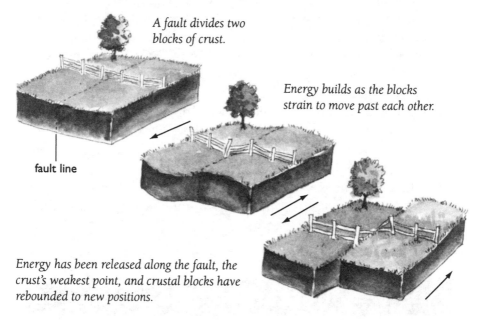

A fault divides two blocks of crust.

Energy builds as the blocks strain to move past each other.

fault line

Energy has been released along the fault, the crust's weakest point, and crustal blocks have rebounded to new positions.

By following directions to fault features and studying them, you can spot them when traveling elsewhere. By following the notes and drawings you make, you can create your own guide to less explored faulted areas. Search in the field for the surface expressions of faults and the damage caused by earthquakes.

1. First, select a guide to the earthquake country you wish to visit. Not all areas of the world are in active earthquake zones; make sure your search for field features is within an area of active seismicity.

2. It helps to have a good guidebook. Follow the leads to determine where to look for earthquake activity.

3. In the earthquake area, look for signs of fault movement by checking for laterally offset features, sag ponds, oases, fault scarps, offset beds in roadcuts, and offset streams.

Model Earthquake Waves

P, or primary, waves create a push-pull effect in rocks. They travel faster than S, or shear, waves. S waves vibrate at right angles to the direction they travel. They create the swaying or rolling motion felt during an earthquake. Recruit a partner to help demonstrate how P and S waves travel through a medium.

1. Tie a small length of yarn to every tenth coil of a spring or Slinky.
2. Holding both ends of the spring, rest it on a counter top or table-top. Then stretch out the spring until you feel some tension. Ask your partner to hold the end of the spring firmly.
3. Abruptly push your end toward your partner, then bring it quickly back into place. Observe the spring and the waves moving through it.
4. Next, hold your end firmly and have your partner snap the spring from side to side. Observe the spring's movement. In which direction did the first wave move? The second? Which wave appeared to move more quickly? What happened to the yarn each time?
5. Repeat several times and observe again.

Study Water's Effect on Erosion

Geology is not all about depositing and creating rock. Many geologic processes are those of erosion, helping to shape the world's landscapes by breaking down rock physically or chemically and moving it else-where. In most environments, rock is both created and destroyed, often in separate areas. Beaches, for example, have areas of deposition, such as where streams lay down sediment near their mouths at the ocean, and areas of erosion, where currents move sand grains from the beach and down the coast or where repeated wave action breaks down the rocky cliffs at the sea's edge.

The type of erosion that occurs in any environment depends on what natural forces are at play. In a river environment the river may cut down into the surrounding rock, and the resulting debris is carried downstream by stream action. In a desert environment with little vegetation to protect sediments from high winds, wind erosion will certainly dominate.

When water moves quickly in a streambed or over a surface of loose sediments, the lighter particles are suspended and carried away in the process of stream erosion. If the water moves quickly and forcefully, even larger particles are affected. A surface will be changed and rearranged, and the sediments will be redeposited wherever the waning currents drop them. You can model the erosive effects of water moving in a stream using a handful of sand and pebbles and a glass jar.

1. Cover the bottom of the jar with the sand and pebbles (fish aquarium rock and marbles may be substituted).
2. Add water to fill the jar three-quarters full. Let the sediment settle for a few minutes.
3. Once the sediment has formed a layer at the bottom, stir the water with the spoon. Be careful not to touch the sediment with the spoon—the idea is to let just the water move the sediment.
4. Begin by stirring slowly. What happens? Now stir faster. Remove the spoon and observe. Make notes and drawings in a notebook.

Stream erosion

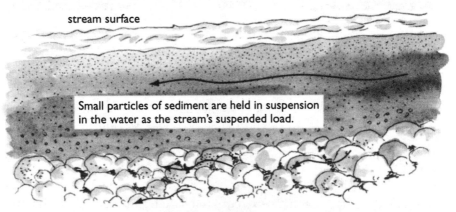

stream surface

Small particles of sediment are held in suspension in the water as the stream's suspended load.

Large particles of sediment—cobbles and boulders— move along the bottom as the stream's bed load.

A cross section of a stream showing how its load is distributed.

5. As the water slows down, what happens to the sediments? Do the lighter or heavier materials drop out of the current first? What happens to the pebbles? What can you conclude about loose material affected by moving water?

Observe Stream Loads

Rocks and debris eroding from side creeks and canyons into a main river channel often spread out into or partially block the current, to form the rocky river passages called rapids. The fine suspended load in creek water may be dropped in its slower passages to blanket the creekbottom. Eroded places include the scoured-out basins of rock that form pools, the cut banks on the outside of meanders, and the edges of sandbars that are carried away with shifts in current.

1. Start by strolling along a creek near your home. If you take off your shoes and walk in the water, you can feel the creekbed with your feet. What features can you feel in the creekbottom? Is it composed of bedrock, pebbles, or sand and mud?
2. You may notice that different stretches have different compositions. If so, sketch the shape and length of the creek and note where bottom changes occur. Does the water appear to carry sediment? Are rocks scattered over the surface of the bed individually or in groups? Where are they with respect to side creeks, pools, the stream current, and the main channel?
3. Create a map of your stream with regard to its current and draw conclusions about how sediments are moved from place to place, thereby undergoing erosion and deposition.
4. If you are able to float down a river by raft or canoe, notice where rapids, pools, and eddies form. Do you see rocks, sediment, and scoured-out places? Where are they in the overall scheme of the river? Are rapids in wide, narrow, or shallow places? Or are they in all three places and more? If so, how do they differ in each place?
5. Look down through the water, and make notes about whether it is free of sediment or full of silt. If you can see any of the river's bed load, sketch it with respect not only to the streambanks but also to side creeks and canyons.

Simulate Wind and Ice

When the wind blows sand against rock, it erodes and abrades the rocks. When water freezes inside rocks, it will expand inside and break the rocks. Both erosive agents are powerful forces in changing the earth's surface. Think about where you see such erosion at work in the field, and watch for similar effects among rocks. You can simulate the effects of wind and ice on rock by collecting and testing a few samples.

1. Gather several rock samples. Make sure you have two samples of each type you collect.

2. Rub together two of the same kind of rock above a piece of paper—if the rocks are light in color, rub them over dark paper; if dark in color, use light paper. Then set the rocks on the paper near the particles that fell. Are the particles the same color as the rocks? Are the rocks scratched where they were rubbed together?

3. Follow the same procedure for each pair of rocks. In your notebook, write your observations, not only about how each set of rocks appeared after rubbing, but how the sets compared. Which rocks created the most particles when rubbed? Which show the most scratches?

4. Next, fill a small glass jar to the top with water. Close the lid of the jar securely and set it inside a freezer-proof container (a bowl or pan tightly covered with foil will work).

5. Leave the jar and container in the freezer overnight. When you remove them later, note the changes that have occurred in the water and glass. Be sure to wear gloves to protect your hands in case anything has broken in the container overnight.

Test Water's Surface Tension

Geologists must understand water and its cycle for several reasons. Water flowing over the ground deposits sand, clay, and gravel, material for sedimentary rocks. Water is also a powerful agent of erosion, shaping and sculpting both soft and hard rock. And some water, groundwater, flows underground, through soil and porous rock. Water is the only substance on earth that exists naturally in all three possible phases a substance can take: solid, liquid, and gas.

Water has many other unusual properties. As a liquid, it can dissolve many hard substances. It has much higher boiling and freezing points than substances with similar molecular structures, such as hydrogen selenide and hydrogen sulfide, two toxic, colorless gases. And upon freezing, whereas other liquids shrink and become more dense, water expands and grows less dense. If it did not, ice would not float on water, and rather than building as a thin skin on top, protecting deeper water from freezing, it would basically freeze from the bottom up. No life could be found in such frozen, solid bodies of water.

The attractive force between water molecules is called cohesion. Because of cohesion, water forms into droplets with distinctive shapes. Also because of cohesion, water molecules cling together in a tough film of skin on water surfaces, a property known as surface tension. Surface tension is important in terms of rock and soil erosion. Because a tough surface skin surrounds each raindrop that falls, drops can hit rocks with enough force to gradually break them down and over time wash them away. You can watch surface tension in action in a few easy experiments.

1. Start by filling a drinking glass to the brim with water. It should be full to the top but not overflowing. One by one, add paper clips gently to the glass of water. Try not to splash and upset the surface. Observe the water surface. Does it stay level? When does the water spill over? Note the results in a notebook.

2. Now set a penny on a table or desk. Guess how many water droplets will fit on the top of the coin before they spill over. Write your estimate in your notebook. Using an eyedropper, transfer water droplets from the glass to the penny. Observe what happens. Do you see

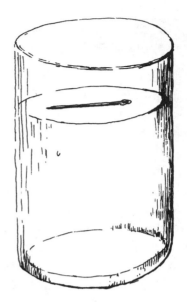

A needle can float on the water's surface due to the tendency of water molecules to stick together.

evidence of a skin forming on the water? Write and sketch the results in your notebook.

3. Next, now that the water level in the glass is somewhat below the rim, carefully float a needle on the surface of the water. Sketch a picture of the floating needle in your notebook. Remember that the needle is made of steel, which weighs more than an equal volume of water. Add a pinch of laundry powder to the glass and watch what happens.

Compare Cohesive Forces

The force that causes molecules to stick together is called cohesion. Compare the cohesive force of some common liquids, such as rubbing alcohol, soapy water, vegetable oil, and tap water. You will need four medicine droppers and a piece of waxed paper about four by six inches.

1. With a medicine dropper, place a drop or two of each liquid on the waxed paper. Be sure to use the same number of drops for each liquid. Which liquid forms the highest heap? The lowest?

2. If a liquid has strong cohesive forces the drop will be high—almost a half sphere. As the cohesive force diminishes, the drop flattens.

How do the drops of these liquids compare? How does the cohesive force of water compare with the cohesive forces of the other liquids? Try this investigation with a thick liquid such as molasses or honey. How does it compare with the liquids you have tested?

3. Fill a glass with water, but do not wet the rim of the glass. With a medicine dropper, very carefully add more water to the glass, drop by drop. Count the drops. How many did you add to the glass that was already full? Eventually a bulge of water will extend above the glass. A "skin" forms on the top of the water due to the cohesive property of water molecules. It prevents the water from spilling over the rim of the glass.

4. Fill a dishpan with about three inches of water. Place a green plastic strawberry container gently on the surface of the water. What happens? To the water, add a few drops of detergent. What happens? What does the detergent do to the surface tension of water? Detergents break down the cohesive force between water molecules. Since these forces were what kept the basket on the surface, the basket does a nosedive.

Test Liquids' Adhesion

Water molecules not only stick to each other, but also will stick to molecules in other objects. This characteristic is called adhesion. Liquids such as honey, vegetable oil, tap water, and soapy water display adhesive qualities. To compare the adhesive qualities of different liquids, you will need to make an incline of waxed paper.

1. Put the edge of the paper on a piece of stiff cardboard, with one edge raised by a couple of books so that the paper slopes downward.

2. Place a drop of each liquid in a row at the top of the waxed paper slope. Describe what happens. Are some of the liquids faster than others?

3. Make a drawing of the path each liquid takes as it moves down the incline. Which liquid has the greatest sticking action? The least? Try this with other liquids.

Explore Density

Density is a science concept that relates closely to our everyday experiences. If you have two same-size solid blocks of wood (or metal or any other material) and one is heavier than the other, the heavier one is more dense. If the block is heavier than an identical block of water, it will sink in water. Minerals dissolved in water increase its density. Salt water, for example, is more dense than an equal volume of fresh water. Temperature also has an effect on the density (weight) of water. The warmer water becomes, the less dense, or lighter in weight, it is.

1. To investigate the effect of mineral matter on the density of water, mix a few tablespoons of salt in a glass half filled with water. Stir to help dissolve the salt.

2. Half fill another glass of similar size and shape with water, and add a few drops of food coloring.

3. Tip the glass holding the salt water and, with a medicine dropper, gently add some of the colored water to the salt solution. What happens?

4. The temperature of water also affects its density. Half fill one glass with hot water and another with cold water.

5. Add a few drops of food coloring to the cold water. Using a medicine dropper, carefully add some of the colored cold water to the hot water. What happens? How does the temperature of the water affect its density?

Investigate Capillary Action

Under certain conditions, the combined forces of adhesion and cohesion work together to create capillary action. Capillary action is one factor that causes water to rise in plants from the roots up through extremely narrow tubes. It is also why cotton and other materials soak up liquids. The properties of adhesion and cohesion of water are constantly at work all around you. Underfoot, the processes move water through the soil, into the layers of decaying leaves, into the cracks in

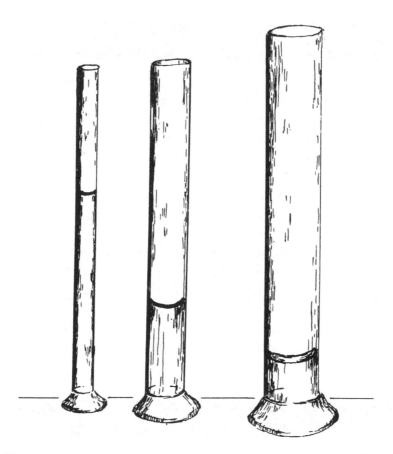

Capillary action at work. The more narrow the tube, the higher the water will rise, up to a point.

the rocks. At every point, life is affected: animal life, insect life, plant life, microbial life.

1. Cut strips of equal length and width (about two inches wide and twelve inches long) from several different brands of paper towels.

2. Tape the strips to the edge of a table or to a cabinet above the kitchen counter.

3. Fill a rectangular container with water, and position it under the strips so that an inch or two of the paper is in the water. Be sure the strips are at the same depth. How high does the water go in each of the strips? How long did it take for the water to reach that height? What do you conclude from this investigation?

Create a Miniature Hydrologic Cycle

The hydrologic cycle is solar powered. No part of the cycle—not ice, rain, surface water, or groundwater—would change without the energy of the sun. Its heat is a great pumping force, driving the lifeblood of the entire planet. No matter where water is in the cycle, whether making its way through soil and rock back to the ocean or whether bound up in ice, the sun's heat assures that water enters the cycle again. You can build your own enclosed hydrologic cycle and watch the process of change. (For more information on the hydrologic cycle, see pages 149–152.)

1. Place two tablespoons of water and an ice cube in a baby food jar.
2. Tape another jar to the first, mouth to mouth, and stand them in a sunny location. Observe what happens to the ice cube and the level of the water. Sketch and note the results.
3. Check the jars each day for a week, noting dates and times along with any observations of what happens inside the jars.

Store Heat

Water absorbs a certain amount of heat without changing temperature. If you've ever burned your hand on the handle of a pot of water set to boil on the stove and noticed that the water inside was still cool, you have experienced the slow effect of increased energy or temperature on a body of water. The opposite process is true for water as well. To cool it down takes more energy than many substances require. So the heat is stored in the water for some time while it slowly gives off energy.

1. Preheat your oven to a low temperature, about 150 degrees. If you cannot use an oven, sunlight will work as a warming agent.
2. Fill one coffee can with soil and another with water. Set them in the preheated oven or sunlight for a few hours.
3. Remove them and measure their temperatures with the thermometer.
4. As they cool, check their changing temperatures with the thermometer. Which cools down faster, the soil or the water?

Float Ice

In its frozen state, water is about 10 percent larger in volume than in its liquid state. It floats in liquid water because it is lighter. The action of water enlarging upon freezing is an important agent of erosion in rock during freeze-thaw cycles.

1. Place two large ice cubes in a glass, and fill it to the top with water, as full as possible without its overflowing. The ice should extend above the water surface and stick up beyond the top of the glass.
2. Sketch a picture. Imagine the ice cubes as tiny icebergs in a small sea. How much of the ice floats? How much is visible above the surface?
3. Observe what happens as the ice melts. The water and the ice cubes did not fit inside the glass, so one would expect the water to overflow the glass as it all becomes liquid. Does it happen? Sketch your results.

Map Shooting Stars

Scientists believe that meteoritic impacts were frequent and severe in the earth's early years. Meteorites penetrated the crust of both earth and moon, causing massive outpourings of basalt, creating magma oceans, and leaving huge impact craters. Today, although major meteoritic collisions are infrequent, astronomers maintain a careful watch of asteroids (and comets, rare sun-orbiting visitors from beyond the orbit of Neptune) that penetrate our solar system deeper than Mars's orbit. Any asteroids that approach this closely are called near-earth asteroids; those three hundred feet or larger in size are considered threatening to life on this planet.

Larger asteroids, five miles or more in diameter, collide with the earth approximately every one hundred million years. Mounting evidence suggests that asteroids impacted the earth sixty-five million years ago, destroying the dinosaurs and most other life forms. One depression found in Mexico's Yucatan Pensisula suggests a meteorite six to twelve miles in diameter hit the earth. The impact of a body that size would have torn a hole in the crust one hundred miles wide, triggered enormous explosions, instigated worldwide earthquakes and tsunamis, and raised huge clouds of dust that blocked the sun and plunged the globe into a freezing darkness.

Most meteors are comet debris, pebble-sized pieces of rock that were once mixed with the ice of comets. Some of these pieces become trapped in cometlike orbits and can remain so for centuries. For several nights each year, the earth encounters these streams of undispersed particles at times that have remained constant over the years. You can conduct your own observation of near-earth meteoroids by mapping meteors, also known as shooting stars.

1. Pick a night that will have a meteor shower (a concentration of thirty or more meteors per hour). Such showers are most likely to occur around August 11 and December 13. You can check the sky watch portion of your local newspaper for information about meteor showers.
2. Dress warmly and sit facing the direction from which the shower should come (this information is also available through sky watch reports). Check the time you begin your observations.
3. Whenever you see a meteor, make a mark in your notebook. At the end of an hour, count the marks. Did you see thirty or more meteors?
4. You can map the meteors on a star chart. Note where each meteor falls with respect to surrounding constellations, and draw a line from the point where it was first visible to the point where it burned out. Mark the leading edge of the line (the direction the meteor was traveling) with an arrowhead. After an hour, check your meteor arrows to see the general direction of travel.

Make Craters

Larger meteorites create larger impacts and larger craters. Create your own impact craters in a baking pan filled with flour.

1. Cover the bottom of a large baking pan with flour, at least half an inch deep.
2. Sprinkle the surface of the flour with colored, powdered paint.
3. Measure and weigh a marble, rubber ball, and golf ball, and then drop each by turns into the flour from a chosen height. You may want to use a string to help you measure the dropping distance above the flour.
4. Using tongs, remove the balls from their craters. Note the physical features of each crater and record all data in your chart. How does the size of the ball affect the size of the crater?

Impact crater

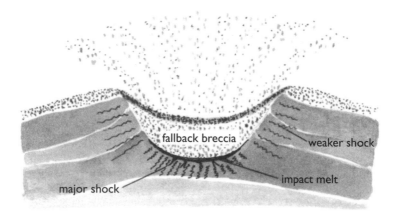

Impact craters have their own peculiar geologic structures, shown here in cross section. Existing layers of rock are disturbed by shock waves and impact melting. Material is ejected from the crater, including earthly rock and fragments of the meteorite that settle around the rim. Broken rock that falls back into the crater is called fallback breccia.

Expand the Universe

It may seem to us on earth that we are at the center of the universe. In truth, however, the universe has no center and no edges. All galaxies are simultaneously moving away from each other. Expansion of the universe began with the big bang billions of years ago. The continued expansion we see today, the moving apart of galaxies, is a relic of that initial propulsion. You can use a balloon to illustrate how the universe has been expanding since the big bang.

1. Place gold star stickers on an uninflated, spherical balloon. Imagine that the stars are really galaxies—some close together, some widely separated. Cluster the galaxies in places and separate them in others.

2. Measure the distances between some of the galaxies. Mark the distances in a notebook and, using a felt pen, mark each galaxy with a corresponding number on the balloon.

3. Blow up the balloon but don't tie it off, as you may want to repeat the experiment. What happens to the galaxies when the balloon increases in size? Measure the distances between marked galaxies while the balloon is inflated. Note that the galaxies themselves do not expand and that no new ones are created.

8

AT THE SEASHORE

Watch Barnacles Feed

Barnacles are clinging, ubiquitous animals of the rocky shore. They're probably best known because of the aggravation they cause saltwater sailors who try to keep boat bottoms clean and slick for the next race. Others who know these animals quite well are barefoot beachcombers. Perhaps you, too, have encountered the cutting edge of the barnacle cone and received wounds that were slow to heal.

Barnacles can be found growing in profusion on the rocks of the intertidal zone. At low tide when the rocks are uncovered, you will notice a distinct white band that appears beneath the black zone where slippery blue-green algae flourish. Look carefully at this white band and you will discover the barnacle colony. Note the location of barnacles relative to the other plants and animals that make their homes on the rocks and boulders of the intertidal zone. You can also look for barnacles in other areas, such as dock pilings and jetties.

1. Find a rock with several barnacles on it, and place it in a bucket containing some seawater. After a few minutes, the barnacles may begin to feed. What do you notice? Use a magnifier to observe the

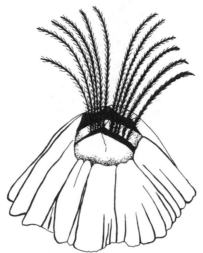

Barnacle feeding

tiny "feet," then describe how they work during the feeding process. How do the plates that cover the opening of the cone function during the feeding process?

2. Do barnacles feed whenever they are covered with seawater, or is their feeding closely bound to the time of high tide? On a day that you can spend some time barnacle watching, check the local newspaper to find out when high tide occurs. At the level of mean high water, find some small barnacle-covered rocks. An hour or so before the incoming tidal waters are due to cover them, put the rocks into a bucket of seawater. When do the barnacles begin to feed? Are barnacles opportunists, grabbing a bite of plankton whenever they get a chance, or does their feeding appear to be closely linked to high tide?

3. How does water temperature affect the rate at which barnacles feed? You can observe their feeding rate by noting how rapidly the barnacles wave their feet in and out of the cone. A good place to observe this action is in a tide pool, since the water remains trapped in the rock pond even at low tide. Take the temperature of the water in a tide pool as the tide begins to fall.

4. At each recorded temperature, count how many times per minute a cone opens and the tiny "feet" sweep the water for plankton. You can count for fifteen seconds and multiply that number by four.

Repeat this several times, and calculate the average rate of sweeping for a specific temperature. Is the feeding rate the same for the other barnacles in the tide pool?

5. Allow some time to pass and then take the temperature of the water in the tide pool again. How do you explain the temperature difference? Find the average feeding rate of barnacles at this new temperature. As the water continues to warm, repeat this process at several different temperatures. What did you discover about the relationship between temperature and the rate at which barnacles feed?

Observe Sea Stars

Of all marine invertebrates (animals without backbones), sea stars are among the best known. Often used as symbols of the seashore, sea stars are usually one of the first animals that come to mind when we think about life along the rocky coast. There is a good reason for their reputation: these cousins of sand dollars and sea urchins are exclusively marine, never found on land or in fresh water.

Your first task will be to obtain a live sea star. Since sea stars must be completely covered by water to survive, you will need to search in shallow water, in the tide pools, and especially on the sides of rocks

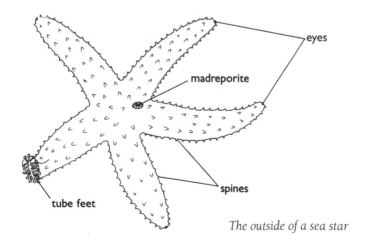

The outside of a sea star

just under the water's surface. Don't forget to look on pilings and along docks and wharves.

1. After thoroughly wetting your hands in seawater, pick up a sea star and put it, prickly side up, in the palm of your hand. With your other hand, rub your fingers along the back of the sea star. The lumps and bumps you feel on the sea star are part of the animal's skeleton. If you gently pinch the rays, or arms, of your sea star, you can feel the calcium carbonate plates that are part of the framework that gives the animal its formal name, echinoderm. This internal structure also provides protection against predators.

2. Try putting the sea star, feet side down, on different surfaces, such as a sturdy piece of smooth plastic, a rough board, or a large piece of sandpaper. These materials should be large enough to provide room for the sea star to move about without falling off. How do these different surfaces affect the manner of movement and the time it takes the sea star to go from one place to another? Does the sea star always lead with the same arm? What do you think determines which arm the sea star will use first?

3. Put a stone in the path of a moving sea star. What does the animal do when it touches the object? Place different objects in its path. What happens? Put a small piece of chicken or dead fish in the path of the sea star. What does the sea star do?

4. On a firm surface, place a sea star feet side up, and observe the animal as it turns over. How long does it take to turn itself over? Does the size of the sea star affect the speed of turnover? What is the role of the tube feet in the somersault? Try the same thing in wet sand. Watch for the tips of the rays to dig into the sand as they aid in the turnover process. Do different species of sea stars turn over in the same way?

5. You have seen how a sea star turns itself right side up, but how does the animal know that it is upside down? Researchers believe that the series of actions that turns a sea star over is stimulated when the tube feet are not touching a surface. You can test this idea by making a cradle out of sturdy thread and suspending the sea star, feet side up. What happens? Now suspend the sea star in a cradle while its feet are toward the ground but still not touching any surface. What happens?

6. With patience and some good luck, you might get to observe a sea star feeding. You could encourage this process by placing some pieces of oysters or mussels in a container of seawater with a sea star. Add a live clam or mussel that's still in its shell. With a bit of luck, you will see the sea star evert its stomach, digest its meal, and "drink" the nutritious liquid. How long does the process take?

Study Slipper Limpets

If you wander among the slippery rocks and seaweed at low tide, you may find, on the smooth surface of a rock, a small stack of beige-colored shells arranged by size. The largest of the shells, perhaps somewhat smaller than the bowl of a teaspoon, is at the bottom of the stack. If you discover this mollusk along the beaches of the Atlantic rocky shore, you have found the common Atlantic slipper shell, or *Crepidula fornicata.*

Another stacking mollusk, the onyx slipper shell (*C. onyx*) can be found south of Monterey, California. Both types of slipper shell animals change sex as they grow, so the larger female is on the bottom, while the smaller males reside toward the top of the stack.

Although there are several types of slipper limpets, probably the first kind you'll notice will be those that are attached to each other in small stacks. To locate slipper limpets, carefully lift the seaweed curtains that cover the rocks, and explore the cracks and crevices of the rocky coast at low tide.

1. With the help of the illustration on the next page, identify the slipper limpet that you found. Did you find the common slipper shell, the convex slipper shell, or the flat slipper shell? At what level of the intertidal zone did you find the different types of slipper limpets? Were they at the high-tide region, the mid-tide region, or the low-tide region? To how many different kinds of substrates or foundations were they attached? What did these foundations have in common?

2. What animals did you find living in the same habitat as your slipper limpets? Make a list of the animals you find and include the approximate number of individuals in each animal group. Which of them occurred most frequently? Least frequently?

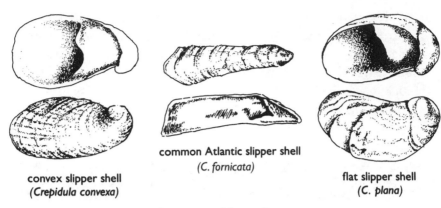

convex slipper shell
(*Crepidula convexa*)

common Atlantic slipper shell
(*C. fornicata*)

flat slipper shell
(*C. plana*)

Three types of slipper limpets

3. Find some stacks of the common slipper limpet or the onyx slipper limpet. How many individuals do you find in each stack? What is the largest number of individuals living together? What was the smallest number of individuals in a stack? Where did you find these stacks? Measure the length of the individuals in each stack. Compare the differences in length of successive individuals in different stacks.

4. Since slipper limpets are attached to a rock by suction, rather than being glued in place like barnacles, some people have thought that they move about. Find a stack of slipper limpets and mark the rock close to them with a small amount of colored nail polish. Observe the stack over a period of several days. Try to go back every few hours during the first day and then once or twice every day for the next few days. What is your conclusion? Try gently to remove a slipper limpet from its foundation or substrate. Would you say that the attachment is firm enough to resist wave action? What other survival advantage is this kind of attachment for the slipper limpet?

Inspect Blue Mussels

Since the rocky shoreline is rhythmically drained every six hours or so, the creatures that make their living here developed unusual adaptations to deal with prolonged exposure to water and wind. Additionally, they have strategies that help them adjust to extreme and rapid changes in temperature, to changes in salinity, to winter storms, to scouring ice, and to crashing waves.

Among the vast array of animals that cope with the rigors of this habitat are blue mussels (*Mytilus edulis*). Their marvelous structural and behavioral adaptations allow them to flourish and to become, at least for a short time, members of the rocky shore climax community. Blue mussels can be found along the Atlantic coast from the Arctic to South Carolina, and from Alaska to Baja California on the Pacific coast.

Look for blue mussels at low tide along the rocky shore where they compete with seaweeds and barnacles for space and food. Also examine pilings and jetties. You will probably notice that blue mussels adhere to a variety of objects by a system of strings or byssal threads.

The byssal threads, or "beards," are one of the most familiar characteristics of blue mussels. Spun by a gland in the animal's foot, the threads serve to anchor the mussels to rocks, to pilings, and even to other stationary animals. With the help of some very strong glue produced by the mussels, the discs hold the mussels firmly in place.

1. As mussels grow, the mantle produces calcium and deposits this new calcium at the wide end of both halves of the shell. The annual

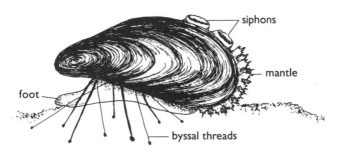

Blue mussel with siphons extended

growth of each mussel is indicated by the width of the distinct wide bands that you see on the outside of the shell. Find a bunch of mussels and measure the width of the last band formed. How much did each of them grow in that year? By counting the number of wide bands, the age of mussels can be determined, although it's difficult to distinguish the bands close to the pointed end. What is the approximate age of some mussels you found?

2. A siphon is a small tube that a mollusk uses to move water in or out. To find the position of the siphons in your mussels, fill a shallow pan with seawater, and submerge the mussels. How long does it take the animal to relax its abductor muscle and open its shell? What differences do you see between the two siphons? Is there a relationship between the diameter of the siphons and the length of the mussels?

3. Through which siphon does the mussel draw in nutrient-rich water? (Which siphon is the incurrent siphon?) And through which siphon does the animal expel water? (Which siphon is the excurrent siphon?) Although you can usually see a turbulence near a siphon as water is expelled from it, try adding a tiny drop of food coloring very near the ingoing siphon to dramatize the currents.

4. Byssal threads are quite strong. To find out how much weight the threads will hold, find a mussel that is attached by a few byssal threads to a small stone. Use a loop of string to attach this stone to the hook of a spring balance with the mussel hanging down supported by its threads. Record its weight. Use Play-Doh or modeling clay to make several small balls of equal size. Stick the balls of clay, one at a time, to the mussel shell and record the total weight. How much weight will the threads hold before breaking?

Collect Seaweeds

Explorers of the rocky shore know that as the tide recedes, horizontal bands are slowly laid bare across the rocks in the thin strip of earth shared by land and sea. The color of the bands is produced, for the most part, by the green, brown, and red seaweeds that live and flourish there.

Scientists call seaweeds primitive plants, because they lack leaves, roots, stems, and other specialized structures found in seed-bearing plants, such as trees and grasses. Because seaweeds possess a different set of special features, they have prospered in their watery habitat for the past five hundred million years.

A good way to begin observing seaweeds is to find some attached to a small rock or mollusk shell. The following activities are centered on whole, living seaweeds that you will find at low tide growing in their natural habitat.

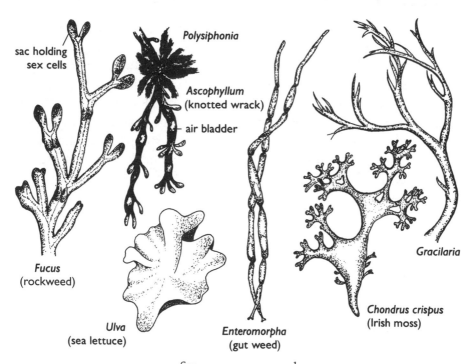

Some common seaweeds

1. Collect about six different types of seaweeds and wrap them in cool, moist paper toweling. You can easily transport your collection in a cooler to a place where you can examine them at your leisure. If it will be some time before you can study them, put the wrapped seaweeds in the refrigerator.
2. How does each different species smell? What color is each of your specimens? Brown, green, olive, pink, purplish red, or some other color? Which color is most common? How does each feel? Soft and flabby? Stiff? Rubbery? Fuzzy? Leathery?
3. Does the thallus, or body, of the seaweed branch? Is it flat like a leaf or stringlike? Is it tubular? Is it thick or thin? Observe the edges, or margins, of the blades of each type of seaweed. Is the margin straight or is it wavy? Is it smooth or toothed?

Dry Seaweeds

You've probably noticed dried seaweed that has been tossed up on the beach and is among the debris stranded there by a high tide. Can seaweeds survive this? Do different kinds of algae dry at the same or different rates? To find out, you will need a fistful of each of three or four different kinds of seaweeds. You will also need a scale, such as a kitchen scale used to measure food portions, and a piece of aluminum foil to hold your seaweeds on the balance pan. If you have to carry the seaweeds some distance from the beach, wrap them in moist paper toweling and store them in a cooler.

1. When you are ready to work with them, remove the seaweeds from their wrappings. Shake and blot excess water from each specimen.
2. Make a little tray out of aluminum foil for the algae. Weigh the tray and record its weight.
3. Place one specimen in the tray on the balance pan and weigh it. To determine the weight of the seaweed, subtract the weight of the empty aluminum tray from the weight of the tray plus the seaweed.
4. Record the weight along with the time and date of the weighing.
5. Proceed in a similar manner for each of your specimens. Then put all of the weighed specimens on a tray and let them dry in direct sunlight.

6. At breakfast, lunch, and dinnertime, weigh the seaweeds and record the weights. Do this until there is no change in weight. For some species, this may take several days. What is the survival advantage to seaweed of this slow drying? You can make a graph that shows the rate of drying for each species of algae.

Make a Snail Aquarium

Periwinkles have been described as unattractive, dirty, dingy, dark, grimy, and even fuliginous. But periwinkles are a large group of small snails that have been inconspicuous, yet successful, residents of the rocky shore community for millions of years. Their genus name, *Littorina*, refers to the zone that lies between the high- and low-water marks at the seashore, where many of these gastropods make their home.

Periwinkles have been studied extensively by scientists investigating the special animal adaptations that are necessary for survival in the intertidal zone. You can begin your study of these interesting animals by observing the common periwinkle, *Littorina littorea*, in your own mini-aquarium.

1. Gently remove a periwinkle from the surface of a rock. Look closely at the opening of the snail's shell. With your fingernail or a small piece of dry grass, very gently touch the disk that covers the opening. How does the snail respond? How does this disk feel?

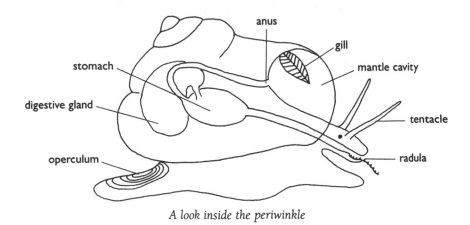

A look inside the periwinkle

2. Select a wide-mouthed jar or bucket. Fill the jar half full of seawater, and add some small stones and some seaweed from the intertidal zone.

3. Leave the jar in a sunny spot for a few days, so that a film of algae can develop on the sides of the jar. To replace the water lost through evaporation, you may have to add some fresh seawater to your jar.

4. You may find that the mini-aquarium will not survive without some aeration, which you can provide with a small aquarium air pump. After a few days, you probably will have many opportunities to see the snail's radula, or rasping tongue, as it scrapes the algae from the sides of the jar.

5. When you observe the mini-aquarium, note how many snails are grazing on the glass above the level of the water. Can you make any inferences about how much of their time they spend out of the water? Do you think this behavior might be related to the amount of time they spend out of the water between low and high tide?

6. You may observe the periwinkles in your mini-aquarium grazing on the surface of the seaweed. They are feeding on microalgae growing on the seaweed. Periwinkles can scrape rocks clean of their algal growth. Their eating activity has also been known to significantly reduce populations of larger seaweeds, such as leafy *Ulva* (sea lettuce) and the tubular strands of *Enteromorpha* (gut weed).

7. While other variables also contribute to a decrease in algal growth on the rocks, periwinkles are probably the primary "lawn mowers" of the intertidal zone. Visit a section of the intertidal zone where there aren't any periwinkles. Do you find a substantial amount of algae and larger seaweeds growing on the rocks? Visit another area where periwinkles are abundant. Assuming that other herbivores are absent or that their numbers are too small to make an impact on the growth of algae, what do you observe to be the effect of periwinkles on algal growth?

Observe Fiddler Crabs

As the tide ebbs along the banks of marsh creeks and drainage canals, hordes of nimble, spiderlike creatures emerge from holes that riddle the peat banks. They scuttle along the mudflats and among the stiff green spears of marsh grass (*Spartina alterniflora*), feasting on the banquet of organic matter so generously served by the sea. These swift, agile creatures are crustaceans called fiddler crabs (*Uca pugnax*). The sun-loving fiddlers are dark brown, making them inconspicuous against the mud they inhabit. Their presence is often first detected by the crackling sounds they make as they scurry to and fro claiming their share of the bounty.

A good place to observe fiddler crabs is in their own habitat while they are going about the business of living. Search at low tide. Look for a stand of salt marsh cordgrass, and you'll undoubtedly find hundreds of tiny crab burrows scattered in the marsh peat. As soon as you arrive, the crabs probably will disappear into their burrows, but if you wait quietly without moving, they'll surface and return to their activities. This is a good time to observe feeding, fighting, and other behaviors. A camera with a telephoto lens will be helpful in recording the variety of behaviors. If you don't have this piece of equipment, a notebook and pencil will do nicely.

The most distinguishing physical feature of the fiddler crab is the oversized claw of the male, which constitutes 40 percent of its body weight.

1. Fiddler eyes are on retractable stalks and are controlled by a complicated set of muscles. Although fiddler crabs cannot distinguish shapes, they are extremely sensitive to movement. How sensitive are these eyes? Sit very still until the crabs are unaware of your presence. With a piece of dead grass in hand, slowly move it toward a crab from behind, from the side, and from in front of the crab. How close can you get before the crab scuttles away? Do crab eyes seem to "see" equally well from all directions? How much movement do you have to make to set off the danger alarm in the group?

2. Do crabs detect vibrations as well as movement? Begin tapping the ground several feet away from the crab. Continue tapping the ground as you move closer to the crab, but be careful to keep all motion to a minimum. How close can you get before the crab scurries away? What are the hunting behaviors of their predators? Which sense do you think the crab uses to detect its predators?

3. Most male fiddler crabs are right-handed: the right claw is the larger of the two claws. It is unusual to find many males whose left claws are oversized, but in some colonies almost half of the males are left-handed. How many left-handed fiddlers do you observe? How many are right-handed? How many crabs have only one claw? What is the relationship between body size and claw length?

Study Horseshoe Crabs

Similar to other arthropods, horseshoe crabs have jointed legs. Additionally they have a hard, inelastic, brown carapace, or external skeleton, that is shed periodically to accommodate the growing animal. In the molting process, which is triggered by hormonal activity, all chitinous parts are shed, even the thin coverings over the eyes and gill books. When the crab emerges, it leaves behind the intact and unmistakable shed for the lucky beachcomber, who often thinks that he has found a dead horseshoe crab.

The horseshoe crab molts by squeezing itself out of its external skeleton, leaving behind the complete exoskeleton, or shed. The exoskeleton splits open along the forward lower edge as the animal

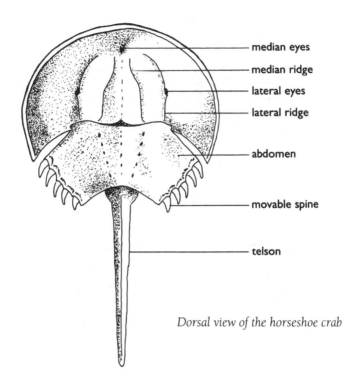

median eyes
median ridge
lateral eyes
lateral ridge

abdomen

movable spine

telson

Dorsal view of the horseshoe crab

emerges. Find a shed on the beach and look for the slit along the leading curve. If you don't find the slit, you'll know you don't have a shed. Instead, you probably have the remains of a dead horseshoe crab.

1. You can use either a shed or a living horseshoe crab to identify the major parts of the animal. Use the accompanying diagram and find the median eyes, the lateral eyes, and the cephalothorax, which is the large portion of the shield. Locate the movable spines on the abdomen and the telson, or tail. Find a living crab to carry the more detailed examination that follows.

2. Using both hands, gently pick up a horseshoe crab by grasping the outer edges of the large shield section. Don't pick it up by its tail! Invert the animal and rest it in the palm of one hand. Although its flailing legs may frighten you, there is no danger from this peaceful creature; it cannot bite, pinch, or sting. Look at the front pincers. How do they differ from the others? What do you think they're used for?

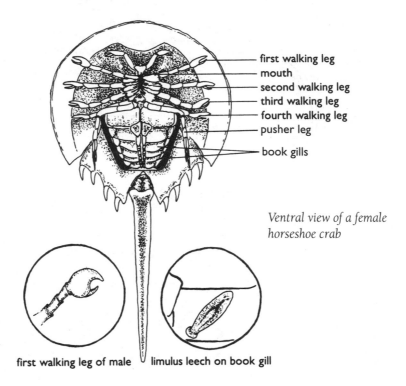

first walking leg
mouth
second walking leg
third walking leg
fourth walking leg
pusher leg

book gills

*Ventral view of a female
horseshoe crab*

first walking leg of male   limulus leech on book gill

3. The first walking legs in male horseshoe crabs are a pair of hooks especially designed for grasping the female carapace. Is your animal a male or female? Find another animal or an intact shed and compare the first sets of claws. Do they indicate a male or female?

4. Look at the last pair of legs. They are especially designed to prevent the crab from sinking into the sand as they shove the animal along in the jerking style characteristic of the moving horseshoe crab. Watch the animal as it makes its way along the beach. Frequently when you return the crab to shallow water, it will immediately attempt to bury itself in the sand. Observe the function of the rear legs in this digging process.

5. Place a horseshoe crab on the sand. Mark the spot where you set it down with a stone or similar object. After one minute, use a tape measure to determine the distance that the crab traveled from the stone. How far did your horseshoe crab travel in one minute? Find several other crabs of about the same size. How far does each of

them travel in one minute? What is their average rate of speed on the sand? Try this with a sample of crabs that are smaller or larger than those in the first group. Does the size of the crab affect the rate of speed on sand?

6. Do you think that the rate of speed would be different if the crabs were moving in the water instead of on the sand? Try it. The receding water often leaves shallow pools on the beach. Place the crab in one of these pools and observe its movements. Does it move sideways underwater? Does it move faster underwater than it does on land?

7. You may find another interesting visitor on the crab. More formally known as *Bdelloura candida*, the limulus leech can be found attached to the undersurface of horseshoe crabs. The worms are not parasites. Instead, they enjoy a commensal relationship with the crab, and this relationship is essential to the worm's life. When removed from the horseshoe crab, the worms don't eat and soon die. Look for these flatworms on several horseshoe crabs. Where do you find them and how many are there in each location? Do they seem to cluster in one or more places? Are they somewhat evenly distributed?

Explore the Eelgrass Community

Eelgrass is not from dry land, nor is it a seaweed. It's a grass, and like all grasses, *Zostera marina* is a flowering plant. Unlike other grasses, eelgrass lives underwater in the shallows that extend beyond the low-tide line. This shallow water often lies behind an offshore sandbar; it provides a buffer zone between the shoreline and the open sea. Here, with a face mask and snorkel, you can explore a gentle, stable community that supports an abundance of life forms.

You are most likely to find eelgrass flourishing in the shoals of protected areas along the Atlantic coast from South Carolina to the Arctic and scattered along the length of the Pacific coast from Alaska to Mexico. While fishing from a small boat or just rowing along the outer edges of a salt marsh, you may see the tips of eelgrass blades poking

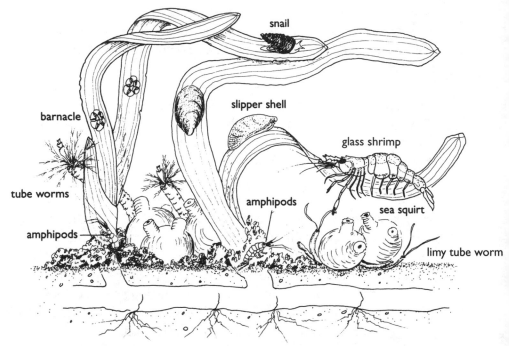

Eelgrass community (not to scale)

above the water's surface as they gently sway to the rhythm of the waves. As you swim slowly over the underwater meadow, using snorkel and mask, you will begin to find creatures of all sizes and shapes. Some of the animals you find will be very mobile, freely swimming among the blades of grass, while others roam very little around the community or may be firmly anchored to the eelgrass. Other groups of life forms live in or on the soft sediment.

1. One group of animals includes all those that graze on the blades of eelgrass. Some members of this group are convex slipper limpets, periwinkles, mud snails, and glass shrimps. You might also see the animals that prey upon these grazers, such as oyster drills and dog whelks. Varieties of ribbon worms, clam worms, and flatworms also find food to their liking on eelgrass.

2. The sediment in the eelgrass community provides shelter for other groups of animals. Some of these beasts live on the sandy mud, while others prefer to make their living while buried in the soft muck. Look for surface dwellers, such as mussels and scallops. To

uncover the indwellers, gently dig up some of the silt with a small trowel. Put this material into a bucket or other suitable container. When you return to your boat, put the sediment into a sieve and flush some seawater through it. What animals do you find living in the muck?

3. Eelgrass blades provide a foundation for many other tiny life forms. Remove some blades of eelgrass and examine them carefully with your hand lens. Using a field guide for assistance, see if you can identify some of the following: sea squirts, hydroids, transparent egg capsules, or sedentary polychaetes, such as *Spirobis* spp., sponges, or bryozoans. Make a separate list of these animals.

4. Make a "larger-than-life" drawing of one eelgrass blade. As you find different plant and animal life forms on the eelgrass, mark your drawing with the location of that living guest of the eelgrass. As you continue your explorations you will develop a "map" showing the sequence of life.

5. The wooden pilings of docks and bulkheads contain the same kinds of animals that you found on eelgrass. Furthermore, the animals occupy relatively similar positions on the blades of grass as they do on the wooden pilings. Find a piling that is host to marine life, and see if you can find those animals you discovered in the eelgrass community. Make a sketch of your piling, and indicate on your drawing, or map, where you found living things. Compare this map with the map of your eelgrass blade. How are the two sequences alike or how are they different?

Examine Bony Fish

Bony fish can be found from the Arctic to the tropics in such diverse habitats as the open ocean, tide pools, brackish streams, and marsh creeks. They come in contrasting sizes, shapes, colors, and behaviors. A trip to the local fish market will reveal some of this variety. There you'll see, side by side, the streamlined torpedo shape of the fast swimming mackerel and wahoo contrasting with the slower moving, flat, pan-shaped flounder, halibut, and sole. Natural selection has worked to design the shape of the flatfish, whose survival is not dependent on speed, but rather on their ability to change color so that they blend with the sandy bottom where they live.

A good way to begin systematic observation is to capture one of the small fish that inhabit the intertidal area and observe its structure and its behavior. It would be better for you to catch two or three fish, each of a different species. If you want to cheat a little, you can get your fish from someone selling "live bait."

1. Put your fish into a clear container large enough for them to swim freely. A wide-mouthed gallon jar usually works well for two or three small fish. Resist the temptation to add more than three small fish to a one-gallon container unless you use an air pump. Add water from their natural habitat until the container is about three-quarters full. Do not use tap water. Keep the container in a bright, sunny area, so that the algae in the water remain alive, but not in direct sunlight, which might cook the fish. Even though this is only a temporary holding tank for your fish, you could add some sea-weed, which will supply oxygen to your system.

2. In making observations of the fish you caught, you probably have noticed the rhythmic opening and closing of your fish's mouth and gills. What is the relationship between the beat of the fish's mouth and that of the gill covers, located behind its eyes?

3. Is there a relationship between the temperature of the water and the rhythmic beats of the gill covers? To find out, put your fish into a container of seawater. Now count the number of gill-cover beats in one minute. (To shorten the procedure, count the gill-cover

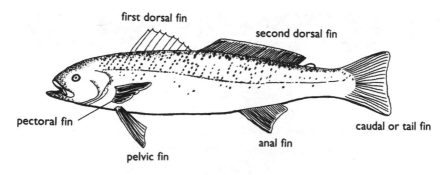

Side view of a bony fish with location of fins

beats for fifteen seconds and multiply that number by four.) Record the number of gill-cover beats. The next step is to lower the temperature of the water. You can do this without diluting the saltwater by adding ice chips that are sealed in a small plastic bag. Drop this package into the water and wait for two minutes. Take the temperature again and record it. Count the number of gill-cover beats at this temperature. As the water continues to cool, repeat the procedure at two-minute intervals. This will not harm the fish.

4. The four nostrils on your fish are used for smelling, but they do not function as breathing organs. Instead, fish use their gill system for breathing. Gills are made up of gill arches, which support gill rakers. These structures trap minute particles in the water that might damage the delicate gill filaments. It's across these filaments that oxygen passes into the blood of the fish and carbon dioxide is removed from the circulating blood.

5. To get a good view of the gills, you can use a fish from the market or a fish head you have obtained from a fisherman. First you should remove the opercula, or gill covers. (Salmon heads are particularly useful for this.) Find the gills and the gill arches. What color are they? How do they feel? Bony fish have four pairs of gills, while sharks have as many as seven pairs. Toxic metals in the water cause the protective mucus secreted by the gill to coagulate, disrupting gill function. Iron, for example, covers the gills with a dense brown coat that interferes with respiration.

Identify Salt Marsh Plants

The salt marsh is home to many plants and animals. It is also a special place where many different species of animals come to mate and raise their young. Disturbing the animals at this critical period in their life cycle could have disastrous results. A careless tide marsh stroller can frighten nesting birds and crush unhatched eggs. Another danger is trampling algae and seed plants that are delicate and sensitive to disturbance. Enter the marsh as unobtrusively as possible and only enough to allow the marsh to teach you its secrets.

   The following activities require that you closely observe other plants that make the marsh their home. Since you will probably need to touch the plants, do so only if you can find them growing beside established pathways in the marsh. Use the following guide to see which of the other common marsh plants you have found.

1. Although most of the dominant plants growing in the marsh resemble grasses, three distinct botanical families are represented. They are the grasses, the sedges, and the rushes. The spartinas are true grasses, because they have hollow, generally round stems with solid bumps, called joints, where the leaves are attached. Another characteristic of grasses is that the veins of the narrow grass leaves run parallel to each other.

2. **Spike Grass.** Look for leaf veins that run parallel to each other. You will also notice that the base of the leaf is wrapped around the stem, while the remainder of the leaf is not. This sheath, often compared to a tube slit down on one side, is a characteristic of grasses.

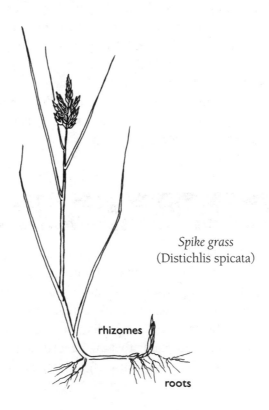

Spike grass
(Distichlis spicata)

rhizomes

roots

Sedge or saltmarsh bulrush (Scirpus robustus)

Spike grass (*Distichlis spicata*) has light green leaves and stiff stems. Also, the dead, curly, tan leaves of last year's growth of spike grass persist close to this year's new growth. Spike grass prefers sandy soil. With the aid of your hand lens, make a drawing of spike grass.

3. **Sedges.** Unlike grass stems, "the stems of sedges have edges." Also, unlike the hollow stems of grasses, the stems of sedges are solid. If you make a horizontal cut through the stem of a sedge, you can see the triangular shape of the stem, which is characteristic of these marsh perennials. You can feel this triangular shape when you roll the stem between your thumb and forefinger. The rhizomes of sedges are food for muskrats and geese, while the seeds are eaten by ducks and other marsh birds. Make a drawing of your sedge and be sure to indicate the differences between it and spike grass.

4. **Rushes.** The zone of the black rush, *Juncus gerardi*, is the highest level of the marsh that saltwater reaches when storm surges and spring tides coincide. Look for juncus in late spring when it is dark green and grasslike. The stem is round, but unlike grasses, there is no node present. If you look for black rush in the fall, you will see

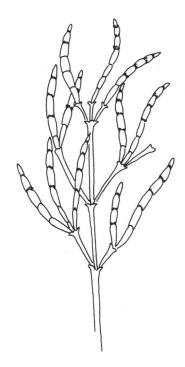

Black grass (Juncus gerardi)   *Jointed glasswort* (Salicornia europaea)

its dark, almost black seeds, which give the plant its common name and make it easy to identify. Another helpful clue is that it grows in dense clumps. Make a drawing of black grass. In March or April, a hand lens will help you to observe the tiny flowers on this rush.

5. **Salicornias.** As you searched the upper marsh for the sedges and rushes, you probably encountered one of the most interesting of marsh plants, the mysterious glasswort. Glassworts of one species or another grow in almost all of our salt marshes. These six- to fifteen-inch plants, fleshy, cactuslike, and smooth, are easy to find. Does the salicornia branch like a small tree as it grows or does it grow in a bunch of single, nonbranching stalks? With the aid of a hand lens, look for the tiny leaves that lie flat against the succulent stems. Sometimes you can find a salicornia that's been uprooted. What kind of root system does it have? What advantage does a succulent have in this environment? Collect as much information as you can from your observations and write a description of the plants.

Examine Mud Snails

Perhaps the animal most closely associated with a mud flat community, especially near the low-tide line, is the eastern mud snail. A careful look at the mud snail's dingy, olive-brown shell, often encrusted with mud and algae, reveals the appropriateness of its name, which comes from Greek and Latin roots meaning "muddy fishing basket." The dilapidated appearance gives a clue to the grueling conditions of life in the intertidal zone. The vast numbers of mud snails found at low tide, frequently as many as a thousand per square meter, is a testimony to their biological success and places them among the major inhabitants of mud flats and other estuarine communities.

Along the edges of these roads and at the bridges over the tidal creeks, you can get a close view of mud flats and even reach into the mud without becoming too muddy yourself. Search the flats for a population of mud snails at low tide.

1. Build a little flag with a toothpick or a bit of straw. Place this "flag" next to a mud snail moving in its natural habitat, or use a natural marker in the mud. Now measure, or estimate, how far the snail goes in five minutes. Repeat this several times and average your results. Based on this figure, calculate how many centimeters per hour constitutes a "snail's pace." Can you calculate a snail's pace in miles per hour?

2. Try to capture a single mud snail without joining the mud flat community yourself. A long, flat stick might help in this task. Put your mud snail on a glass pie plate or a piece of clear, colorless plastic.

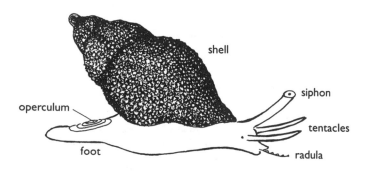

Mud snail (Illyanassa obsoleta)

Looking from below this platform, observe the rhythmic contractions of the snail's foot. Does the mud snail leave a mucous trail on the glass? How might that help the snail's forward movement?

3. With the aid of your hand lens, find the tentacles, eyes, and siphon of the mud snail. Gently touch the snail's head with an object such as a tiny piece of straw. What did the snail do? Touch it with your finger. Does it react in the same way or differently? How does the mud snail react when it bumps into an object like a stone or a small stick?

4. The next step is to observe a group of mud snails. This is a logical step because mud snails frequently feed in groups. To investigate this behavior, gather about six mud snails, put them on a clean pie plate, and observe them moving around the plate for five minutes or so. Do they tend to stay isolated or do they tend to form one or more groups? Make a sketch as a record of what they do. Carefully remove them.

5. Next place one new snail on the plate. Observe the movements of this snail on the plate. Does it move randomly or does it move in the same direction as the original group did? Does this mud snail seem to follow the trails left by the other mud snails? What you are observing is a mud snail's response to chemicals left by members of its own species. What advantage is this chemoreception for mud snails?

Identify Shore Birds

The smallest of the warm-blooded animals to make a living from the intertidal zone, shore birds take advantage of the enormous number of beach fleas, worms, mollusks, crabs, and other invertebrates that make their homes on and under the sand and mudflats. It's been estimated that as many as thirty-five hundred of these invertebrates live in every square meter of a sandbar, while the same area of the more organic mudflats supports over eight thousand of these energy-rich tidbits.

At first glance, all of the little birds that flock to the sand and mudflats to feed look distressingly alike. However, if you spend some time

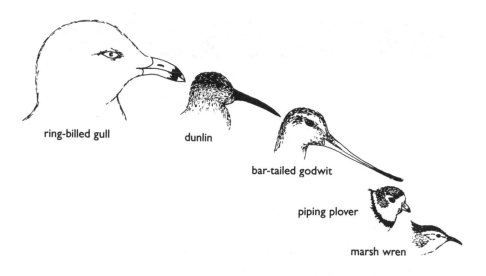

ring-billed gull

dunlin

bar-tailed godwit

piping plover

marsh wren

Observing bill shape and size is one way to identify a variety of shore birds.

watching them, the job of deciding who's who in the world of these birds will become much less confusing. You'll find that a field guide will be easier to use if you first learn to observe the birds' general features and then to make behavioral observations.

1. Select an intertidal habitat, such as a mudflat or salt marsh, and make yourself comfortable without being intrusive. For a few minutes, observe the many different kinds of birds that come to the area.

2. At first, don't try to observe every detail; just see if you can divide the birds into two or three different groups of similar birds. What cues did you use to put the birds into the different groups? Usually, the first thing you tend to notice is size—big birds and little birds.

3. If you persist, you will notice other differences: bills, necks, legs, tails, shape, and markings, like neck or beak rings. As you keep looking, you'll notice a variety of distinctive behaviors, such as walking versus running and unusual feeding motions.

Identify Bird Tracks

Bird tracks make an interesting study. Among the best places to find them are on sandy beaches near the water's edge or on mudflats at low tide.

1. Select an area. How many sets of tracks can you find? How many different kinds of birds made the tracks? Which type of tracks are the most frequent?

2. Select a series of tracks that you think were made by one bird. How far apart are the tracks? What do you think the bird was doing? Hopping? Walking? Running?

3. Look for evidence of a bird's pecking and probing in the sand. Where do you find the most evidence of feeding? Close to the swash line, near the strand line, or other places?

4. Select a set of tracks. Make a map to show the path a bird traveled across the mud or sand. Select another set of tracks. Using a different color, make another path map. What do these maps tell you? Use a compass to determine the primary direction in which the birds traveled. How far did each bird move in that direction? In what other directions did the birds travel and for what distance? What was the greatest distance each bird traveled from the time it landed on the sand until its tracks were no longer discernible?

5. Observe a variety of birds as they walk in the sand or mud. When they fly off, observe and draw their distinctive tracks. With the combined help of your field guide and your own observations, find out the names of these birds. If you develop the ability to identify a bird solely from its tracks, you are on your way to becoming a beach bird expert!

Take the Pulse of a Mud Worm

Worms found in the intertidal zone can be grouped in a variety of ways. One method used to classify them is according to their food-getting habits. In this system, errant, or wandering, polychaetes make one group, while sedentary polychaetes form the other.

Members of the wanderers, or errant polychaetes, leave their burrows in search of food.

Most of these worms are meat eaters with biting jaws appropriate to this lifestyle, but they won't hurt you if you are careful when collecting them. One of the most common wandering polychaetes is the clam worm, or *Nereis*. You'll often find them wriggling in tide pools or in intertidal shallows. Their opalescent sheens or rich copper reds and browns make identification relatively simple, especially when you observe the bristles on their many side feet, or parapodia.

The stay-at-home cousins of the errant polychaetes are the sedentary polychaetes. These worms live most of their lives inside tubes that they build from a mix of sand and bits of broken shells glued together with mucus secreted by the worm. With the aid of a face mask or a glass-bottom bucket, you can observe the worms feeding in the shallows of the intertidal zone. Make these observations while the tide is up. Among the most exquisite are the terebellid worms, which can be found from the Gulf of St. Lawrence to the tropics.

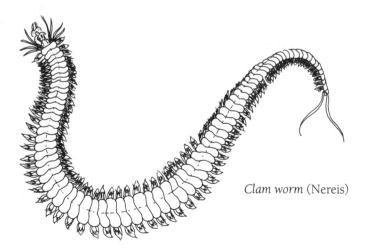

Clam worm (Nereis)

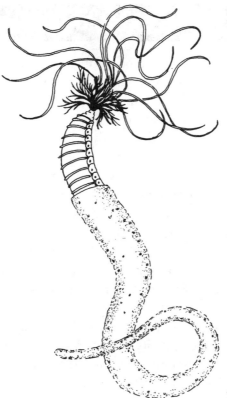

Terebellid worm (Thelepus)

Polychaetes live in an ever changing environment. You can discover how one of these environmental variables affects the worms by experimenting with changes in temperature. The clam worm is a good subject for this investigation, because it is easy to observe the expansion and contraction of a blood vessel located along the back of the worm. The vessel appears as a dark wavy line along the dorsal, or top, side of the worm as the vessel fills and expands; the vessel disappears under the skin when it contracts and empties. Thus the animal's pulse rate can be counted.

1. You may find that this counting requires careful observation through your hand lens and the extra light of a flashlight held close to the worm. You also may need a helper with a watch to count and time the beats as you call them out. To determine the pulse rate per minute, simply count the beats for fifteen seconds and multiply

that number by four. The beat may be more obvious at the tail end of the worm.

2. In order to control the temperature of your worm, find a spot in which to work that is out of direct sunlight, since you do not want the sun to interfere. Put a small amount of water and some chipped ice into a small Ziploc bag. After you have counted the pulse rate at room temperature, put your worm on the cold plastic bag and count again several times.

3. You can test the effect of higher temperatures by adding warm water to a plastic bag. How is the pulse rate of the worm affected by temperature? When you're finished with the worm, be sure to return it to its habitat.

Build a Worm Aquarium

You can unearth polychaetes by gently digging mud from around their burrow openings. Put the mud you collect onto a sieve (window screening will do nicely), and sift out the sand and mud particles. You may need to wash some sea water over the surface of your sieve. The worms will remain behind, and you'll be able to observe them in your aquarium.

1. Put about three inches of sandy mud into a large mayonnaise jar.

2. Cover the mud with a sheet of waxed paper and pour seawater into the jar.

3. Remove the waxed paper. The covering on the mud will prevent it from mixing with the water and making your system murky.

4. To supply necessary oxygen to the water, you can buy a bubbler, a pump, and some plastic tubing from an aquarium supply shop at minimal cost. The equipment can be used again for other watery habitats that you might want to build.

5. As you acquire marine worms, you can add them to the mini-habitat and make observations over a period of time.

Distinguish Sand Particles

Perhaps the most familiar characteristic of a beach is sand, and though all sandy beaches look the same from a distance, they can actually be very different. For example, upon close examination, minerals such as the light tan feldspar and glistening quartz grains from the beaches of Long Island's south shore or New Jersey's shore contrast sharply with the stark white coral grain from the beaches of Florida and the Keys. Pick up a small handful of sand and look at it closely with a magnifier. What you see will depend very much on where you are, because sand is not one thing, but many things, which can be as different as oranges and bananas! In all sands you will probably see individual grains in a variety of colors, shapes, and sizes. If your sand sample is from a beach in the Northeast those tiny particles, some perhaps millions of years old, have been eroded from granite and other igneous (fire born) rock formations. Because of the origin of the particles, you'll probably see fragments that look like tiny pieces of glass. With their sharp corners rounded from thousands of years of weathering, you are undoubtedly looking at quartz.

1. Observe the sand from different areas of the beach, such as the foreshore, the berm, and the back beach (see the diagram). What is the relationship between particle size and the distance from the

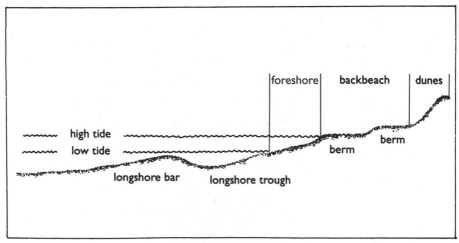

Profile of a sandy beach

water's edge? What is the relationship between the slope of the beach and particle size? What are some of the generalizations you can make about the size of the sand particles and their location on the beach?

2. Make your own sand collection by obtaining clean baby food jars with lids. Label each jar with the date, the location of the beach, and the part of the beach from which the sand came. You will also want to include the wave action, such as the wave height and time between waves breaking on the shore. Some of the sand you collect will need to be washed with fresh water to remove particles of silt and bits of organic debris. Dry the sand by spreading it on sheets of plastic. Be sure to label the drying sheets to avoid a mix-up when you return each sample to its container.

3. If your friends travel to coastal regions different from the places you visit, ask them to bring you a small sample of sand from those beaches. Be sure you tell them how to label the collecting jars. This is a good way for you to get sand from beaches along the Atlantic and Pacific coasts as well as from the Gulf of Mexico.

4. Depending on its origin, sand can be divided into two groups. If it comes from the breakdown of animal skeletons, shells of mollusks, bits of coral, and pieces of sea urchin spines, it is referred to as biological sand. If the sand is the result of weathering and erosion of rocks, it is called nonbiological sand. Put about one-half teaspoon of sand on a piece of dark colored paper and examine it with a hand lens. What shapes and colors are the sand grains? What size are the sand particles? Are the grains flat? Do they have sharp edges? Are there bits and pieces of shells in the sample? Are there grains of different colors? What minerals do you think are in the sand sample?

5. Biological sands contain animal remains, such as crab carapaces, mollusk shells, and sea urchin spines. These exoskeletons are made of calcium carbonate. To find out whether or not your sand has biological origins, put a few drops of vinegar on a pinch of sand. Calcium carbonate will react with acidic vinegar by forming bubbles of carbon dioxide. Since nonbiological sand will contain some calcium carbonate particles, you must observe this reaction closely with your hand lens. Are only a few particles reacting with the vinegar or is the reaction a general reaction among almost all the sand particles?

Sample the Strand Line

A line of debris often running parallel to the water's edge, marking the line of high tide is commonly called a wrack line, or strand line. This line is made of material that's been "stranded" by tidal waters or storm waves. The strand line contains materials that once floated in the sea, carried by winds and currents. This debris may have traveled only a few miles or it may have journeyed several thousands of miles from its place of origin.

1. Walk along the strand line of your beach and examine its contents at regular intervals, every ten feet or so.
2. Make a tally sheet of everything you find in it.
3. Sort the material into groups. Do you have anything that is of human origin such as Styrofoam cups, plastic plates, pieces of rope, or fishing line? Are there any signs of animal life, like shells, egg cases, or crab or lobster sheds? Is there any evidence of plant life, such as driftwood or eelgrass? Do you find a variety of seaweeds? Does one particular type of seaweed seem to predominate?
4. Identify the various objects that you found in the strand line. What did you find most often? What was rarely found? Which of your groups had the most material? Which had the least? Transfer this information to a chart and see if you can find any relationships.

Explore Beach Zonation

Although zonation is much less obvious on the beach than in other intertidal habitats, bands of life exist from mean high water to mean low water. Tide, salinity, exposure, and the shifting of the sand affect what organisms are found. So that your exploration of the intertidal beach is not haphazard, use the method described below to discover the variety of life and its distribution in the beach habitat.

1. Make a transect by laying a string or a clothesline from the splash zone (see illustration) to the water's edge, securing each end of the line with a rock or other heavy object.

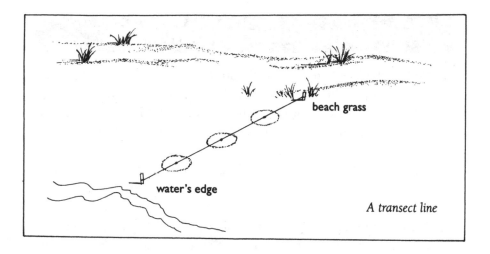

beach grass

water's edge

A transect line

2. Tie knots at regular intervals along this line.
3. With a knot as its center, you can scribe a circle in the sand using a piece of string six inches long. Do this at each knot, so that you will have a series of circles, each with a diameter of twelve inches. If you prefer, you can use a wire coat hanger to form the circles, placing it at each knot as you work your way down the transect line.
4. Beginning at the top of the splash zone, examine each of the circles along the transect by carefully digging up the sand to look for any living things that might be there.
5. Spread the sand onto a flat sheet of plastic, gently separating the particles. What do you find? Dig deeper. What do you find at this new depth?
6. At each circle along the transect, examine the sand and dig to the same depth as you did before.
7. Keep a record of what you find and how many of each living thing there are in each location. Where did you find the greatest number and greatest variety of living things and where did you find the least? How do you explain your findings? Use a field guide to identify the living things you found.

Identify Beach Animal Life

1. **Beach Fleas.** A common inhabitant of the strand line is the beach flea, from the *Orchestia* genus. These agile tan or olive scavengers feed on decaying plant and animal material. When captured and examined with the aid of a hand lens, beach fleas look like tiny shrimp and show many of the characteristics of amphipods, including jointed legs and segmented bodies. How many body segments can you find? How many legs? What do you think dines on these fleas of the night?

2. **Ghost Crabs.** Relatives of the fiddler crabs, these agile beach animals have the formidable name of *Ocypode quadrata*. Often the only sign of their presence is a hole in the sand that marks the entrance to their burrows. Ghost crabs remain beneath the sand during the heat of the day and venture out only at dusk, at night, and at dawn. Since their colors very closely match those of the sand, ghost crabs are very difficult to see as they run across the beach in search of a meal. See if you can discover how they are adapted to life in the upper beach. Based on your observations, what role do these animals have in food chains?

3. **Mole Crabs.** This fascinating member of the mid-Atlantic beach community makes its home in the most unstable, turbulent habitat, where few animals and no plants can exist. They are egg shaped, and have the color and texture of an egg. They have no pincer claws, and the legs and other parts fold flat against the body. When they feed, they dig in the lower part of their bodies facing away from the waves. The antennae capture very tiny bits of food from the rushing water. When you attempt to capture one, it will dig itself out of sight in a flash. How many special adaptations to their special beach niche can you identify?

4. **Coquina Clams.** Although the tiny coquina clam (*Donax variabilis*) is only about one-half-inch across, it is very active. On the high-energy sandy beaches south of Cape Hatteras on the Atlantic coast, you will not find any mole crabs. Instead, you will find the coquina clam. The coquina feeds the same way that the mole crab does. It uses its strong foot to move up and down the beach with the tide,

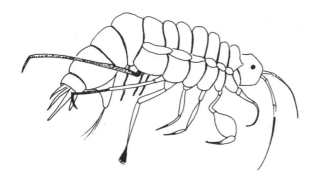

Beach flea
(Orchestia agilis)

Ghost crab
(Ocypode quadrata)

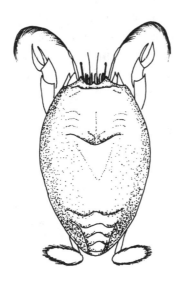

Mole crab
(Emerita talpoida)

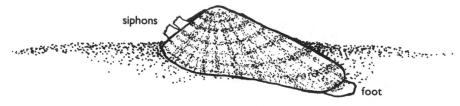

Coquina clam (Donax variabilis)

so that it stays in the swash zone. Like the mole crab, it is a filter feeder, feeding as the wave washes back down the sand. It can dig into the sand very quickly. You will be surprised at the great variety of colors and patterns that mark the coquina shell.

Measure Sand Temperature in a Dune System

Born of sea, sand, and wind, extensive dune systems occur most frequently along the beaches of the barrier islands that stretch intermittently along our coastline. The wide and gently sloping continental shelf contributes considerable amounts of sand to the construction of these dunes. Washed onto the beach by the sea, the sand dries, accumulates, and is moved around by the wind. When the sand-laden wind meets an object such as a piece of driftwood or other debris, it slows down and drops some of its freight of fine sand. Grain piles on top of grain, and slowly a small sand mound builds. From this meager beginning, the wind, a skillful artisan, crafts the dune. As the pile of sand increases in height and width, it offers more resistance to the wind, and a steady supply of new sand for the developing dune is guaranteed.

To begin your observations of a dune system, find a place where you can get an overview of the dune field. You will notice that the sequence of these sand hills is more or less parallel to the water's edge. You will also observe that the vegetation from the foredune landward is arranged in horizontal bands, or zones, that are distinguished by changes in plant color from light to dark green and by changes in plant density from sparsely settled to thickly vegetated.

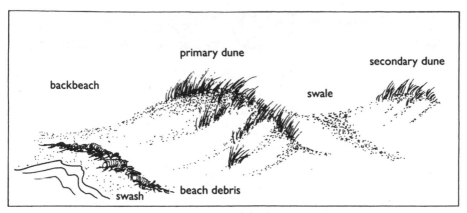

Dune sequence

1. Use a thermometer to measure the temperature of the sand on the front of the primary dune, the back of the primary dune, in the swale, and on the front and back of the secondary dune. You will need to begin early in the morning so that you can get a complete pattern of temperature variation during the day. (You can damage your thermometer if its range is too narrow, so be sure that it reads to 100°C.)

2. You should take several temperature readings in each location and find the average. At hourly intervals throughout the day, repeat the procedure.

3. In the evening when you have finished, you can put your information for each location on a separate graph. This will show you the relationship between the time of the day and the temperature in each of the above places in the dune field. How do the temperatures change during the day? Do they change proportionally from one region to another? Does one area get disproportionately hot during the day? How do you explain these temperature variations?

Explore Plant Variety in the Dunes

How does the variety of plant species in the dune field change as the distance from the water-and-salt-laden wind increases? One way to find out is to make a transect across the dunes.

1. Lay a clothesline from the beach to the back of the secondary dunes.
2. Make a three-by-three-foot square from a few wire hangers.
3. To sample plant life in your dune system, lay the quadrat across the clothesline every five feet or at any other workable, regular interval. Begin at the face of the primary dune and follow your transect landward.
4. Each time you lay your square on the transect, record the number of plant species in it. You will also want to record the number of individual plants of each species in the quadrat. Which plant type is most dense? Which plant is least dense in each quadrat?
5. As you progress from the foredune to the back of a secondary dune, how does the variety of plant life change? Is there a greater number of different plant types? Where is the variety of plant life the greatest? Where is variety the least? Are some plant species found in all of the quadrats? Do you find any sea oats or beach grass on the back of the secondary dune?

Measure Temperature below the Sand

By measuring the temperature of sand below the surface, you can discover how different creatures are able to survive in this harsh environment.

1. Take the temperature of the surface sand in a swale.
2. Now dig into the sand about two inches and find the temperature in the hole.
3. Continue digging in four-inch increments, taking the temperature at each four-inch depth until you've dug a hole about two feet deep.

4. How did the temperature change as you dug into the sand? What are the implications of your findings for animal life in the dunes? Why is there an apparent absence of animals on the surface of the sand during the day?

Measure Temperature above the Sand

How does the temperature of the air change at increasing distances above the sand? To find out you will need a long pole such as a broom handle.

1. Tape several thermometers at regular intervals along the pole, beginning several inches from the bottom.
2. Stick the pole, with its thermometers, into the ground. What happens to the temperature of the air as the distance above the sand increases?
3. Chart your results and be sure to include the time of day, the wind speed, the humidity, the color of the sand, and the shape of the dunes facing the swale. Why is the color of the sand an important consideration affecting the temperature above it?

Identify Animals in the Dunes

The animals that live in the dunes are almost all arthropods, such as insects and spiders, and many of them can be seen during the day. Dune-dwelling vertebrates like mice tend to stay in the cool protection of their burrows by day, venturing out only in the cool of the evening or before dawn.

1. With the help of a field guide, find some of these curious dune dwellers. Velvet ants (which are really wasps), sand-dwelling grasshoppers, digger wasps, tiger beetles, and ant lions are only a few of these rugged insects.

2. Take some time observing them and see if you can discover some of their survival adaptations.

3. If your search for animal life is in an area that has extensive dune fields, you will find evidence of the presence of a variety of species of higher animals, such as birds, snakes, lizards, turtles, raccoons, foxes, toads, meadow voles, and white-footed mice. However, you will not find frogs or worms. Why not?

Follow the Tides

Until very recently, the phases of the moon and the ebb and flow of the tide were an important part of daily life for mankind. For farming and hunting peoples, the passage of the moon through its phases marked off the year like a monthly calendar in the sky. The moon signaled the time to plant and to hunt, the time to fish and to harvest. The question "What time is high tide?" is as important today as it was in days past for those who live near the sea and draw their living from it and for those who enjoy catching an occasional seafood meal. Certain species of fish

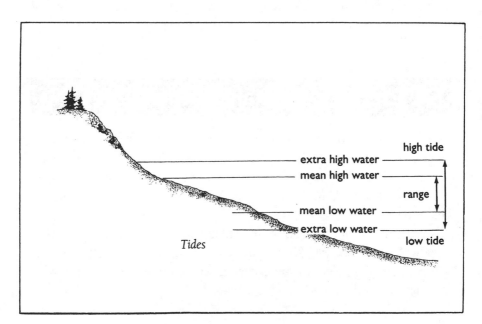

Tides

and crabs can be caught on the turn of the tide, while others are best caught at high tide.

If you visit several different coastal areas and take pictures at high tide and again at low tide, you can begin a pictorial record of these changes. It is essential for you to take the pictures from the same place on each beach at both high and low tides. If you prefer, you can make drawings instead of taking photos of the beaches. Regardless of the method you choose to record the changes in the shape of the shoreline, be sure you include in your records the name of the beach, date, time, phase of the moon, and weather conditions.

1. When you go to the beach, bring a stick about five feet long. A broom handle with one end sharpened will do nicely. Find a place that is away from the crowds and away from swimmers. Pound the stick firmly into the sand at the water's edge with a rock, and with a rubber band, mark the stick at the level of the water (the highest wet spot will do). Record the time and wait a little while. Then check the water level on your stick. Is the tide flooding (coming in) or is the tide ebbing (going out)?

2. If the tide is falling, place your stick at the highest spot reached by the most recent wave. Then keep moving your stick back to the edge of the water every half hour. Observe the time when the tide stops falling. Was there an in-between time when the tide stayed quiet without moving out or moving in? Note the time when the tide begins to move in.

3. As the tide rises, use rubber bands to mark the height of the tide on your stick every half hour. You will want to keep track of the time as each new rubber band goes in place until the tide reaches its highest mark. How high is the high tide above the low tide? What portion of its total rise did the tide rise the first hour, second hour, and third hour? Did the tide rise evenly or in spurts? At what portion of the tidal cycle was the maximum rate of rise? What happened to the rate of tidal rise during the next three hours?